D0465057

realSEX

For Christie —

real SEX

the naked truth about chastity

Enjoy!!

LAUREN F. WINNER

*Lauren F. Winner
October 2005*

Brazos Press
Grand Rapids, Michigan

Published by Brazos Press
a division of Baker Publishing Group
P.O. Box 6287, Grand Rapids, MI 49516-6287

Printed in the United States of America

Library of Congress Cataloging-in-Publication Data
Winner, Lauren F.
    Real sex : the naked truth about chastity / Lauren Winner.
        p.   cm.
    Includes bibliographical references.
    ISBN 1-58743-069-X (cloth)
    1. Chastity. 2. Sex—Religious aspects—Christianity. I. Title.
BV4647.C5W56 2005
241'.66—dc22   2004022537

This book is dedicated to the worshiping community
of Christ Episcopal Church
in Charlottesville, Virginia

\Chas"ti*ty\, n. [F. chastet['e], fr. L. castitas, fr. castus.]
1. The state of being chaste; purity of body; freedom from
unlawful sexual intercourse.

— www.dictionary.com

Chastity is the most unpopular of the Christian virtues.

— C. S. Lewis

CONTENTS

I

UNCHASTE CONFESSIONS

Or, Why We Need Another Book about Sex

Confession is a romantic form, not least because it presupposes that sin is still possible.

—Stacy D'Erasmo

Chastity: it is one of those unabashedly churchy words. It is one of the words the church uses to call Christians to do something hard, something unpopular. It is a word that can set our teeth on edge, and it is the topic of this small book.

Chastity is one of the many Christian practices that are at odds with the dictates of our surrounding, secular culture. It challenges the movies we watch, the magazines we read, the songs we listen to. It runs counter to the way many of our non-Christian friends organize their lives. It strikes most secular folk as curious (at best), strange, backwards, repressed.

Chastity is also something that many of us Christians have to learn. I had to learn chastity because I became a Christian as an adult, after my sexual expectations and mores were already

partly formed. But even many folks who grow up in good
Christian homes, attending good Christian schools, and hanging out with good Christian friends—even these Christians-
from-the-cradle often need to learn chastity, because unchaste
assumptions govern so much of contemporary society.

I am not an expert on chastity. I am not a theologian or a
member of the clergy. I'm just a fellow pilgrim. What follows in
this book is no more and no less than one person's reflections
on the process of learning to practice chastity. I don't offer
instructions or hard-and-fast rules. Instead, I offer a flawed
example, a few suggestions, some thoughts about what works
and what doesn't work, and the occasional reminder of why, as
Christians, we should care about chastity in the first place.

An Autobiographical Excursion

My own history with chastity is nothing to be proud of. I
first had sex when I was fifteen, with a guy I met at summer
camp. We dated for three months, and had sex, but gradually
our relationship dissolved—he went away to college, we wrote
letters occasionally, but things fizzled out. A year later, I started
college myself. And even though I was part of an observant
Jewish community, I kept having sex. My freshman year, I dated
a stunning man (he looked like an Armani model), and we had
sex a few times. Then I began dating the man I now think of
as "my college boyfriend," and we had sex too. None of this
behavior was sanctioned by my Jewish community, so I kept
it pretty quiet. I didn't have communal approval, but through
secrecy I managed to avoid outright censure.

And then, near the end of college, I began to explore Christianity. I popped in and out of churches. I spent time with the
Book of Common Prayer. I read Christian novels. (In one, the
second in the Mitford series by Jan Karon, the author makes
clear that the unmarried characters are not having sex. "Since
we've never discussed it, I want to say that I really do believe
in doing things the old-fashioned way when it comes to love,"

explains Cynthia, a fifty-something divorcee, to her beau, an Episcopal priest. "I do love you very dearly and want everything to be right and simple and good, and yes, pleasing to God. This is why I'm willing to wait for the kind of intimacy that most people favor having as soon as they've shaken hands." "How quaint!" I thought. "Abstinence! Between members of the AARP!")

As I graduated from college and moved from New York to England for graduate school, I got pretty serious about Christianity, and about Jesus. I was going to church regularly by then, praying to Jesus, thinking about Him as I walked down the street, believing with a certainty that surprised me that He was who He said He was: God. I did some of the things you might expect someone who believes that Jesus is God to do. I got baptized. I started spending inordinate numbers of hours hanging around with other Christians. I read the Gospels. I prayed the psalms. I wore a small silver cross around my neck, proclaiming to passersby that I was part of this tribe whose allegiance was to Jesus. I knew that I was falling in love with this carpenter who had died for my sins.

But there were other things that you might expect a Christian to do, and I did not do them. (You might especially expect a Christian who had been an observant Jew and was therefore used to discipline, rigor, and religious authority to do these things, but still I did not do them.) I didn't forswear sex. I didn't tithe. I didn't especially enjoy going to church on Sunday mornings; in general, I had to grit my teeth, silence my alarm clock, and drag myself there.

I knew, dimly, that Christianity didn't look kindly on premarital sex, but I couldn't have told you very much about where Christian teachings about sex came from. I did read the letters of Paul, but to tell you the whole truth, I wasn't entirely sure what "fornication" meant, or how much leeway I had in interpreting it. In fact, I'd never even actually heard the word "fornication" before reading the New Testament—it certainly wasn't common parlance among grad students at Cambridge University. I knew it had something to do with illicit sex, but

I wasn't sure exactly what constituted illicit sex. Also, there was the problem of translations—what appeared as "fornication" in some Bibles appeared as the even more vague "sexual immorality" in others, which left me only with the ill-defined sense that the Christian God cared somehow about how His people ordered their sex lives.

It would not have been too difficult, of course, to get more clarity on this sex issue. I could have looked up "fornication" in the dictionary. Or I could have picked up any number of books designed to help readers just like me, new Christians, figure out the basics of Christian living. I didn't do those things for two reasons. First, sex was not immediately on my radar screen, as I hadn't met anyone I wanted to go to the movies with, much less go to bed with. Second, perhaps more important, I didn't really want to get more clarity on Christian sexual ethics, because I wanted, should the opportunity arise, the option of having sex.

So instead of digging deeper into the question of Christianity and sex, I settled for an easy conclusion: what God really cared about was that people not have sex that might be harmful in some way, sex that was clearly meaningless, loveless, casual. Yes, the context for sex mattered, but marriage might not be the only appropriate context. As long as everyone involved was honest, no false promises were made, no one got hurt; as long as sex was a sign of love and commitment, surely God would approve or, at least, not disapprove. That seemed doable—give up the occasional night of drunken revelry with some cute, random guy you met at a party, and reserve sex for truly committed relationships.

I more or less managed to abide by that. I didn't have sex until that truly committed relationship came along, and then when it did—when I met a man I'll call Q.—I did. Once, during the Q. months, I broke my own pledge, to God and to Q., having sex one night with an ex-boyfriend and then lying to Q. about it. I began to have some twinges of misgiving and went to talk to a minister I knew slightly, Pastor H. That conversation didn't get me very far. In hindsight, the best thing

Pastor H. could have done was direct me to another pastor. Tucked away in a small country parish outside Cambridge, Pastor H. spent most of his time dealing with geriatrics, not twenty-somethings, and the last time he'd been asked directly about sex outside marriage may have been around the time the Beatles recorded *The Yellow Submarine*. Still, Pastor H. tried to rise to the challenge, and over a cup of Lady Grey tea, he said that the church forbade premarital sex because Paul was clear about it in the Bible. Then he scribbled down a few verses on a sheet of heavy cream paper, and sent me on my way.

But the twinges continued (even after the "committed relationship" with Q. ended and another "committed relationship" began) and eventually I went to another priest, in America this time, to formally say confession. I was there to confess a long litany of sins, not just sexual sin—lies I'd told, ways I'd screwed up friendships, a whole host of mistakes and missteps. Somewhere in the middle of that confession I came to the sexual sin, and my confessor said, gently but firmly (which are the two adverbs I now believe should apply to any Christian rebuke), "Well, Lauren, that's sin."

And in that sacramental moment, kneeling with another Christian whose sole task was to convey Christ's grace and absolution to me, something sunk in. I still couldn't have given a solid disquisition on sexual ethics in the Pauline epistles, but I knew that this priest had just told me something true.

I wish I could say that at that moment with my confessor everything changed, that I abandoned all that smacked of sexual sin and never looked back; but that's not true. What happened, instead, was that I had a failure of nerve. I suggested to my current boyfriend that we stop having sex, he balked, and so we continued to have sex. Shortly thereafter, we broke up, and I began what has been a sometimes-halting movement deeper into chastity.

The beginnings of chastity, for me, required a number of things. I began a much more serious examination of what scripture has to say about sex (more about that in the next chapter). I read a lot of popular Christian books about sexuality, some of which suited and many of which disappointed me. I prayed. I had good, if sometimes hard and embarrassing, conversations with Christian mentors. Sometimes I slipped up, and then I prayed more and had more hard conversations. Sometimes I lay on my bed and stared at the ceiling and wondered why this mattered. And occasionally, I understood very well indeed why it mattered.

Chastity is not always easy or fun. (Once I was standing in front of my car with my then-beau, E. His arms were wrapped around my waist and I kissed his cheek and said, "So, I think we're doing pretty well on the chastity front, don't you?" and he allowed that yes, he thought so too, and then he grinned in that way he sometimes has and said, "Maybe too well.") Which is to say that being chaste is sometimes strange, and difficult, and curious. But it is also a discipline, and like any spiritual discipline, it gets easier and better with time.

Looking back, I think it is absolutely appropriate that I began to understand something about sex while at confession. The rite of confession is, to my mind, the most mysterious and inexplicable of the Christian disciplines. In fact, many Christians do not observe a formal order of confession at all. I have never really understood intellectually what happens at confession; rather, I have taken on faith that in the confessional God's grace is uniquely present, regardless of my ability to articulate why or how. So it is fitting that in that moment full of grace I made a real beginning of chastity, because it is only God's grace—and not my intellectual apprehension of the whys and wherefores of Christian sexual ethics—that has tutored me in chastity.

Sexual Sin and Contemporary Christendom: A Report Card for the Church

That's the brief outline, and it skips a lot: a lot of frustration, a lot of backsliding and not-so-upright behavior, a lot of trying to figure out what, exactly, chastity means, and why God cares when we do and do not have sex. Before I presume that readers want to bear with my explorations of chastity, I owe you a word about why I wrote this book. There are, after all, many books about Christian sexual behavior, about "waiting till marriage," about preserving one's purity, and so forth.

I did not write this book because I want to challenge or overhaul the traditional Christian teachings about sex, but rather because I want to challenge the way the church typically helps people practice those teachings. I have, by now, read countless books and heard countless lectures on singleness, chastity, and refraining from premarital sex. Many of these lectures and books seem out of touch with reality. They seem naïve. They seem designed for people who get married right out of college. They seem theologically vacuous. Above all, they seem dishonest. They seem dishonest because they make chastity sound easy. They make it sound instantly rewarding. They make it sound sweet and obvious.

What's honest is this: chastity is God's very best for us. God created sex for marriage and that is where it belongs. Still, many Christians who *know about* chastity have a hard time *being* chaste. Chastity may *be* instantly rewarding, but it doesn't always *feel* instantly rewarding, and, let's face it, we live in a therapeutic culture in which people often make decisions based on what seems to feel right at the time. Too often the church, rather than giving unmarried Christians useful tools and thick theologies to help us live chastely, instead tosses off a few bromides—"True love waits" is not that compelling when you're twenty-nine and have been waiting, and wonder what, really, you're waiting for.

The church is falling short somewhere. We say we care tremendously about premarital chastity, but somehow the tools we give people to live premarital chastity are not working as well as we might hope. I know my own story of sex and sin and chastity is not necessarily representative. But both studies and anecdotes suggest that I am not alone in struggling with sexual sin.

About 65 percent of America's teens have sex by the time they finish high school, and teenage "dating" websites like hotornot.com and facethejury.com (which boast, respectively, 4.3 million and 1.2 million members) encourage teenage patrons to select not prom dates but partners for casual sexual escapades. A 2002 study by the Centers for Disease Control and Prevention found that 41 percent of American women aged fifteen to forty-four have, at some point, cohabited with a man. According to the 2000 census, the number of unmarried couples living together has increased tenfold between 1960 and 2000, and 72 percent between 1990 and 2000. Fifty-two percent of American women have sex before turning eighteen, and 75 percent have sex before they get married. According to a 2002 study by the Kaiser Family Foundation and *Seventeen* magazine, over a quarter of fifteen- to seventeen-year-old girls say that sexual intercourse is "almost always" or "most of the time" part of a "casual relationship."

Christian communities aren't immune from the sexual revolution. Statistics on unmarried Christians and sex are both hard to come by and not wholly reliable—people tend to fudge when talking to pollsters, presenting their lives as they wish they were, not as they actually are, so the single Christian talking to a pollster may pretty things up a bit. Still, a few snapshots from the field:

Three surveys of single Christians conducted in the 1990s turned up a lot of premarital sex: approximately one-third of the respondents were virgins—that means, of course, that two-thirds were not.

Recently professors at Albion College and Illinois State University surveyed 200 college virgins to learn why these folks hadn't had sex. When offered a list of thirteen possible reasons for abstinence, most of those surveyed said the main reason they'd remained chaste was that "I haven't been in love or been in a primary relationship long enough." Religious reasons came much lower on the list, seventh for women, ninth for men—suggesting that people are abstaining from sex not principally because they find the Christian story compelling, but because they find a popular tale about romance compelling—*wait till you've really fallen in love.*

True Love Waits, a popular Christian abstinence program with roots in the Southern Baptist Convention, was founded in 1993. The program asks teens to make the following pledge: "Believing that true love waits, I make a commitment to God, myself, my family, my friends, my future mate and my future children to be sexually abstinent from this day until the day I enter a biblical marriage relationsip." In 2001, a study of 6,800 students showed that virgins who took the pledge were likely to abstain from sex for eighteen months longer than those who did not take the pledge. This was touted as good news by abstinence advocates, but actually it is troubling—it means simply that a lot of abstinence pledgers are having sex at nineteen instead of eighteen. This is hardly a decisive victory for abstinence. As one reporter summarized the findings, "The pledge was more effective among 16-year-olds than 18-year-olds; there was no entirely conclusive evidence about its effectiveness among 15-year-olds; and it was only effective among those surveyed so long as less than 30 percent of their classmates took it. It had to be popular, but not too popular. Pity the poor policy maker who's supposed to act on these findings, navigating the incomprehensible logic of high-school cliques and identity politics." The study, which was conducted by sociologists at Columbia and Yale, also showed that students who broke the pledge were less likely than their non-pledging peers to use birth control—presumably in part because the use of birth control implies that one thought about sex beforehand; one *planned* for it; but the culture among Christian singles dictates that the sin is somehow less grave if one got swept up in the heat of the moment.

In 2003, researchers at Northern Kentucky University showed that 61 percent of students who signed sexual-abstinence commitment cards broke their pledges. Of the remaining 39 percent who kept their pledges, 55 percent said they'd had oral sex, and did not consider oral sex to be sex. (Anecdotally, a roughly equivalent percentage of self-identified evangelical college students I recently spent the day with said they didn't consider anal intercourse to be sex.)

Luke Witte, an evangelical Presbyterian pastor at Forest Hill Church in Charlotte, North Carolina, says he asks engaged couples to cease having sex before their wedding. "I won't marry a couple who is sexually active," he insists. "There are biblical reasons. We're asked not to fornicate." But Witte, interviewed for a 2002 *New York Times* article, acknowledged that he has to have the chastity talk with most of the engaged couples who ask him to marry them. "More than not," he says, "there's a sexual relationship" before the couple ties the knot.

Vanderbilt University, like many colleges, features a sex column in its student newspaper. The woman who writes Vandy's column—which has recently covered such topics as anal sex, bisexual experimentation, and the extra zing that tongue rings lend to oral sex—is a regular at an evangelical student ministry. In a column where she mentioned scripture, she offered a winking, parenthetical acknowledgement of the irony: "I was at [an evangelical Bible study] this past Wednesday (that is correct, I, . . . the sex columnist, do study the Bible)."

In 1992, flagship evangelical magazine *Christianity Today* surveyed over one thousand of its readers. Forty percent said they'd had premarital sex. Fourteen percent said they'd had an affair. Of those who had cheated on their spouses, 75 percent were Christians at the time of the affair.

One might hope that the strongest predictor of teenage virginity would be church involvement—but it's not. A recent study of teenage girls shows that the strongest predictor is actually participation in team sports. The girl who plays lacrosse or soccer is more likely to remain chaste than the girl who attends church and youth group. Apparently sporting leagues are doing something right, and the church is (so to speak) dropping the ball.

I wanted to get a sense of how the struggles of single Christians to stay chaste were playing out in my neighborhood, so I spoke to Greg Thompson, a campus pastor with the Reformed University Fellowship at the University of Virginia. Charlottesville is, in many ways, a pretty conservative place. I thought if any corner of the church would exemplify chastity, it might be here. It seems I was wrong. Greg said that with one exception, every dating couple he has counseled has "talked about sexual failure." Most of these dating couples, he said, are "having serious problems understanding what to do and what not to do with their sexuality. . . . I consistently have conversations with Christian students who are either having sexual intercourse, or having oral sex, or taking their clothes off and masturbating each other. Every college pastor I've talked to about this says the same thing: their students, even those in their leadership groups, people leading Bible studies and so forth, are sexually out of control."

Many other campus ministers report similar dismay at the current sexual scene. As one pastor at another large Southern school put it, "Most of my students struggle with sex. Many are having sex with their boyfriends or girlfriends. Some are even prone to one-night stands. . . . At best, my students 'mess up' frequently (i.e., every month up to every few days) and wrestle with the guilt that comes with such episodes of making out (whether intercourse is involved or not), but rationalize their physical intimacy as 'OK.' Those students who aren't sleeping around want to and are bitter. I used to be optimistic about this, but I am seeing fewer and fewer students hold on to purity and chastity. . . . If you ask me, it all comes back to the implications of the authority of scripture (of course, there are other factors). They don't get it, so they don't apply it. . . . Sometimes I wonder if I'm living in Amos 8:11–12 every time I step on the college campus." I did not happen to have Amos 8:11–12 committed to memory, so I looked it up.

It says: "'The days are coming,' declares the Sovereign LORD, 'when I will send a famine through the land—not a famine of food or a thirst for water, but a famine of hearing the words of the LORD. Men will stagger from sea to sea and wander from north to east, searching for the word of the LORD, but they will not find it.'"

The Place of Experience in Christian Ethics

Because this is a book about ethics, and because this is a book about experience, I want to make one thing clear at the outset. To yoke ethics and experience is not to imply that one's ethics should be derived primarily from experience. A Christian ethic may, in cases, take experience into account, but Christians ground their ethics—their behavior—foremost in scripture and tradition.

There are, to be sure, some instances where experience—the church's experience of living the church's narrative in a fallen world—significantly informs a Christian ethic. Take domestic violence. A careful reading of scripture suggests that Christians are forbidden to divorce except in two cases—when one spouse has committed adultery, and when an unbelieving spouse abandons a believing spouse. But compassionate Christian communities, wrestling with a problem that may not have parsed in first-century Palestine, may well want to suggest that a wife whose husband beats her can legitimately divorce. As biblical scholar Richard Hays puts it in *The Moral Vision of the New Testament*, "The physical violence of spousal abuse [may] constitute another circumstance that would justify marital separation, even though the New Testament does not address this problem directly."

In the main, however, experience considered apart from scripture and church tradition is not a very firm basis for ethics, for the simple reason of original sin. Our individual experience is corrupted; thus it must be interpreted by and refined by Christian scripture and tradition.

I experience the church's teaching about sex as difficult. I chafe against it. Sometimes it feels outmoded, irrelevant, burdensome. But to rely on my experience here would be to rely on something frankly broken and distorted. Sometimes it is scary or inconvenient to trust the church. But it is more often a relief to know that I don't have to rely solely on my intuition or experience to make decisions about ethical behavior. The church is here to teach me how to handle sex, money, time, relationships, and myriad other issues.

So, if my point in bringing together ethics and experience is not to say, "Oh, in the twenty-first century, these teachings are just too hard; let's toss scripture and tradition out the window and embrace fornication"—why, then, talk about people's lived experience at all? Is doing so a concession to the voyeuristic tell-all that characterizes so much of today's popular culture? I think not. For if our ethics of sex should not be primarily grounded in experience, our pastoral response to sex must take account of it. By *pastoral*, I mean something broader than simply what clergy do; I mean the compassionate and wise response of all brothers and sisters in the Christian community to those siblings in Christ struggling with questions of sex and chastity.

We Christians insist that bodies and what we do with them are important. We insist that sex was created for marriage alone, and that unmarried Christians shouldn't have sex. But if we want to do more than insist—if we want to help those unmarried Christians inhabit chastity—we ought to know something about what role sex plays in their lives.

Put another way: one of the best books I have read about sex is Lewis Smedes's *Sex for Christians*. It is a superb book. It is clear, it is straightforward, it is compassionate. But it was written the year I was born. Is it still useful? Absolutely. I recommend you go out today and buy a copy. But it's also a little dated. Smedes wrote in the heyday of the sexual revolution. He wrote in the midst of a tremendous social transformation. He wrote when the broader culture's attitude toward sex was still in flux. Today very little is in flux. The sexual mores that were still radical and challenging in 1976 have gelled (indeed, they may seem a bit tame: Smedes speaks of "petting," but the vocabulary with which we speak of sex has changed so dramatically that I am not entirely sure what that term denotes). Smedes wrote for an audience that still remembered something of a "traditional" sexual ethic. I write for those of us who have no memory of chastity.

What I mean to say is that there is a difference between sociology and theology, literally the difference between the study of people and the study of God. When it comes to matters sexual, the church has devoted centuries, tomes, vats of ink to the theology and ethics of sex. But our sociology of sex is weaker, skimpier. If we want to help our single folk hew to chastity, we ought to know how they think about, and how they enact, sex and chastity. We need to know what lies behind the familiar euphemism, "Chastity is something I struggle with."

Tools for the Journey

There may be skeptics who, reading along, think, *She's really spending too much time stressing how hard chastity is. Just zip up your skirt and be done with it.*

But the point is not to harp on how difficult chastity is. (Indeed, the instruction to *just zip* perhaps fails to recognize that one resists strong bodily urges like sexual desire not primarily through willpower, but through grace.) The point is that chastity, like most aspects of the Christian life, does not come naturally, and that the church might do well to think intentionally about the resources it can offer for educating people into chastity, and sustaining them in the midst of chastity.

One ingredient in my own moving toward chastity was *time*, months and years of growing as a Christian. For, though I was baptized and confessing the name of Jesus at twenty-one, the process of living into Christianity, of being formed in Christian ways, is a long process, a life-long process. I say this not to excuse the sins of those new to the faith (and certainly not my own sins), but rather to remember what, in church-speak, we sometimes call *discipleship* and sometimes call *formation*. Something very dramatic and transformative happens when a person becomes a Christian, when a person is born again or baptized and gives her life to Jesus and the church. But conversion makes one a *new* Christian, not a mature one, and though it effects a change in one's heart and one's very being, it does not usually effect an instantaneous change in all one's habits or assumptions. In the early church, catechumens often took three years to prepare for baptism, precisely because new patterns of living take time to establish. In my own case, I became a Christian when I learned one very basic, true thing—that Jesus was God Himself, and that He had died to save me from my sins. There were, after that first lesson, still many things to learn—or, more to the point, to relearn. I had to relearn how to pray, how to interact with my family, how to spend money, how to use my time, how to comport my body, how to understand my work. Learning those new Christian habits took time. Indeed, it is still going on.

In my attempts to live chastely, *prayer* has been key. It may sound hokey, but I have prayed regularly that God would reshape my heart and my desires so that I would want the things He wants for me. And every day, I have prayed about sexuality when saying the line from the Lord's prayer, *Lead us not into temptation*. Of course, "temptation" doesn't refer just to sex, but for most unmarried Christians, sex is right up there on the list of temptations worth avoiding.

And (you may as well know upfront that I am an unreconstructed bookworm) *reading* has helped—reading the Bible, of course, but also ranging around Christian classics, the fathers and mothers of church history, whose accumulated wisdom about chastity offers a robust alternative to the confused messages our contemporary society sends us about sex.

Finally, a most important key ingredient: *the church*. The church—by which I mean the body of believers, rather than the buildings and pews they inhabit on Sundays—is part and parcel of that formation and discipleship of which I spoke ear-

lier. We, one another's siblings in Christ, are meant to instruct
and nurture, and we are also meant to reprimand and hold accountable. To be honest, in my own walk with chastity I have
learned the importance of the church as much by the church's
absence as by its presence. Sometimes I have been bowled over
by the harm the church has done—in my life and others'—by
speaking thoughtlessly, or not speaking at all, about sex. But
other times I have been stunned by the generosity and compas-
sion and firmness fellow Christians have shown me as I have
wrestled with chastity and sexual sin. Like my confessor, they
have quite simply spoken truth in love.

What You'll Find in These Pages

A few words about what this book is, and what it is not. Its
focus is on premarital chastity, and it is part of a specifically
Christian conversation. My goal is not to convert the broader
culture to chastity (though if secular folk pick up this book and
are inspired, fantastic), but rather to provide companionship
and strength for the journey for unmarried people who are
trying to live in a Christian moral universe. As such, I do not
spend much time making social-scientific arguments against
premarital sex: I won't remind you that sexual promiscuity
leads to STDs or an increased risk of cervical cancer, for example, or argue that premarital sex does violence to the weave
of our social fabric, though both those things are true. Nor
will I tackle issues like adultery, homosexuality, and divorce,
though those are all topics that a comprehensive account of
Christian sexual ethics would need to address.

But you will find that I talk, not infrequently, about
marriage.

This book took me much longer to write than I originally
anticipated. Finding an idiom and a voice for discussing sex
and chastity in a way that was honest but not alienating proved
harder than I thought. Indeed, being up-front and frank about
my own sexual sin has proved harder than I expected, too, for

it is not something about which I feel cavalier; to the contrary, I still feel real shame about having had premarital sex.

Then while I was writing this book, a funny and unexpected thing happened. I met a man named Griff, and we began dating, and nine months later we got engaged, and six months after that we got married. So a book that began as one "swinging single" talking to another evolved into something slightly different (though not that different; as I send the book off to the publisher, I've been married exactly three-and-a-half months).

The changes in my own autobiography, however, do not account for my discussions of marriage. Initially, I set out not to mention marriage at all in this book. For many of my own single years, I cringed when Christians talked about marriage. I was sick of hearing about nuptial bliss, sick of feeling as if I wasn't participating in authentic Christian life because I wasn't married, sick of feeling inferior to everyone who happened to be a wife. *The book I write*, I thought, *won't have any of that. It will be the real deal about singleness, and it won't make anyone feel icky by prattling on about marriage.*

But as I wrote, even before I met Griff, I realized there was a good reason that Christian conversations about sex often circle back to marriage. What sits at the center of Christian sexual ethics is not a negative view of sex; the Christian vision of marriage is not, at its most concise, merely "no sex before marriage." Rather, the heart of the Christian story about sex is a vigorously positive statement: sex was created for marriage. Without a robust account of the Christian vision of sex within marriage, the Christian insistence that unmarried folks refrain from sex just doesn't make any sense. And so I had to change my tack and write more about marriage than I had originally planned. I write about marriage because the core of this book is an effort to offer a definition, in a Christian vocabulary and grammar, of good sex, even (as the title suggests) of real sex. I seek to set out the characteristics of good sex, and to explore who partakes of it, under what circumstances.

I don't pretend to have a magic formula for ensuring premarital chastity. What I share in this book are some tools I wish

I'd had sooner. My reflections come not only from my own experience, but from two years of conversations with pastors and counselors and lots and lots of single Christians. What resources, I asked them, do you wish you had to live chastely, or to help people live chastely? I have tried to gather together their wish-list of resources and put them all in one place. And so, though this book focuses on the topic of premarital chastity, it is not written only for the unmarried, for living chastely is a communal endeavor, one that requires the participation of the entire Christian community. And this book is also written for the whole Christian community because, if premarital chastity is my central topic, I also write about married sex. What does our belief that sex belongs in marriage teach us about what good married sex looks like? This question shadows the entire book, especially chapters three, four, and five.

Real Sex is divided, loosely, into two halves. The first half is a study in thinking about sex and chastity. What is the biblical view of sex? What messages do we get from the broader culture about sex, and how, given the biblical account of sex, should we evaluate those messages? The second half is much more practical. Chastity is tough; how do we—as individual Christians, and as a Christian community—go about being chaste? You will find that I have tried to articulate both the biblical vision of sex and the honest difficulties of living in this vision; I have tried to sketch both the tragedy of living outside the biblical vision and the hope for living within its bounds. And I have tried to evoke the beauty of desire, the beauty of how things were made.

To begin that evocation, we turn to scripture, the place where a Christian understanding of sex and chastity starts.

PART
ONE

‖‖‖

TALKING
ABOUT SEX

2

REAL SEX

Creation, Scripture,
and the Case for Sex in Marriage

Good sermons and good books are of excellent use, but yet they
can serve no other end but that we practise the plain doctrines
of scripture.

—Jeremy Taylor

The bottom line is this: God created sex for marriage, and
within a Christian moral vocabulary, it is impossible to defend
sex outside of marriage. To more liberal readers, schooled on a
generation of Christian ethics written in the wake of the sexual
revolution, this may sound like old-fashioned hooey, but it is
the simple, if sometimes difficult, truth.

For several years, I tried and tried to find a way to wiggle
out of the church's traditional teaching that God requires chastity outside of marriage, and I failed. I read all the classics of
1970s Christian sexual ethics, all the appealing and comforting
books that insisted that Christians must avoid not sex outside

of marriage, but rather exploitative sex, or sex where you run the risk of getting hurt. These books suggest that it is not marriage per se, but rather the intent or state of mind of the people involved, that determines whether or not sex is good and appropriate; if a man and woman love each other, if they are committed to each other, or, for Pete's sake, if they are just honest with each other about their fling being a no-strings-at-tached, one-night stand, then sex between them is just fine. After all, as long as our 1970s man and woman care about each other, making love will be meaningful. In fact, sex might even liberate them, or facilitate their personal development.

Well. I tried to find these books persuasive. I wanted to find them persuasive. I wanted someone to explain to me that I could be a faithful Christian and blithely continue having premarital sex. But in the end, I was never able to square sex outside of marriage with the Christian story about God, redemption, and human bodies.

It wasn't just the liberal, supposedly liberating, books that left me cold. I didn't find many of the more conservative bromides all that persuasive either—the easy proof-texting that purports to draw a coherent sexual ethic from a few verses of Paul. To be sure, scripture has plenty to teach us about how rightly to order our sexual lives, but, as the church, we need to ask whether the starting point for a scriptural witness on sex is the isolated quotation of "thou shalt not," or whether a scriptural ethic of sex begins instead with the totality of the Bible, the narrative of God's redeeming love and humanity's attempt to reflect that through our institutions and practices. If our aim is to construct a rule book, perhaps the cut-and-paste approach to scripture is adequate: as the bumper sticker wisdom goes, *Jesus* (or in this case, Paul) *said it, I do it*. But if we see scripture not merely as a code of behavior but as a map of God's reality, and if we take seriously the pastoral task of helping unmarried Christians live chastely, the church needs not merely to recite decontextualized Bible verses, but to ground our ethic in the faithful living of the fullness of the gospel. As ethicist Thomas E. Breidenthal once put it, "We must do more than invoke the will of God if we wish to recover a viable Christian sexual morality. . . . Even if God's will is obvious, it cannot provide a rationale for any moral code until we are able to say, clearly and simply, how God's command speaks to us, how and why it addresses us not only as a demand but as good news."

Remember my visit to Pastor H., the English minister who jotted down a few snippets from Paul and sent me on my way? In the narrowest sense Pastor H. was right. The church derives its sexual ethic from scripture, and Paul has a few sharp-tongued things to say about sexual morality. But (as you know from reading chapter one) those verses of Paul had little impact on me. That is probably more my failing than anyone else's, but for a few-months-old Christian—too Christianly young to be said to be formed in Christian virtues and hardly eager to stop sleeping with her boyfriend—an isolated verse from 1 Thessalonians was about the easiest thing in the world to ignore. In the narrowest sense Pastor H. had explained to me why premarital sex was out, but in a broader sense, he had explained nothing at all.

An analogy may help make the point. If my sexual habits were formed by Hollywood and *Cosmo* and therefore at odds with how Christianity would have me comport my sexual self, my shopping habits were equally schooled in a surrounding secular culture whose assumptions are contrary to those of the gospel. Compact discs were coming into fashion when I was in fourth grade, and my father, upon buying a CD player, presented my sister and me with one CD each—Leanne got ABBA's greatest hits, I got the more modish Madonna, her album *Like a Virgin* (which may itself speak volumes about how I was formed sexually) with its hit single, "Material Girl." And though after college I eschewed lucrative job offers to work on Wall Street and rake in more money than a twenty-one-year-old should be allowed to earn, I nonetheless was something of a material girl. I liked to shop. I owned a lot of silk blouses. I was singularly unreflective when it came to matters of money, ownership, and wealth.

Not that I hadn't read the Gospels, where Jesus has quite a few things to say about money, ownership, and wealth. I had read his strict words about the rich man's inability to get into heaven. I had even heard sermons that quoted these lines and urged the faithful to be "good stewards," whatever that meant. (As far as I knew, a steward was a male airplane attendant.)

Jesus's words did, in fact, lodge like small burrs in my side, and I began to feel pangs of something—though I'm not quite sure you could call it guilt—when I went on those silk shopping sprees. But it was not until I began to grasp the larger arc of the Gospels' teaching about wealth and possessions that the radical nature of Jesus's words began to sink in. It would be a dramatic overstatement to say that today I am a model of simplicity (I do still own a few silk tops), but I have begun to take steps toward simple living, and those steps were goaded not merely by hearing Jesus's harsh words to the rich young ruler, but by hearing them through the scrim of centuries of church teaching on ownership and possession, by coming to see how Jesus's words were not isolated instructions but integrally related to basic Christian themes of creation, ownership, and salvation.

As with wealth, so too with bodies. Yes, St. Paul's sexual guidelines would be sufficient. But they would be sufficient the way a black-and-white film clip is sufficient. Sometimes you see gospel truths in very sharp relief when they are just in black and white. But sometimes they are clearer and more arresting when they are seen not as isolated instructions, but rather as part of the large biblical narrative of creation, fall, and redemption—the entire story in Technicolor.

Christian Bodies

God made us with bodies; that is how we begin to know that He cares how we order our sexual lives. There is—and we will walk through it here—evidence aplenty from both scripture and tradition about how God intends sex, about where sex belongs and where it is disordered, about when sex is righteous and when it is sinful. But the starting point is this: God created us with bodies; God Himself incarnated in a human body; Jesus was raised again from the dead with a body; and one day we too will be resurrected with our bodies. That is the beginning of any Christian ethic—any moral theology—of how human beings in bodies interact with other bodies.

Sexuality touches every area of human life; even something as simple as a kiss can have social consequences (after The Kiss, you go from being the girl next door to being his girlfriend) and emotional consequences (you hadn't realized you liked him *that way* until then). Kisses can play on our psychological and spiritual registers. But sexuality, even mere kissing, is also, unavoidably, bodily. After all, we define a kiss by body parts: a kiss happens when lips meet a cheek or a hand, or when two sets of lips rub up against each other. Kissing can make our bodies tingle. And kisses can be slobbery; like other sexual deeds, they are messy in their embodiment.

So an investigation of God's vision for human sexuality would begin with God's vision for human bodies. And that investigation can be less simple than it seems. The Christian story, at its core, has very positive things to say about bodies, but throughout its history the church has sometimes equivocated. We Christians get embarrassed about our bodies. We are not always sure that God likes them very much. We are not sure whether bodies are good or bad; it follows that we are not sure whether sex is good or bad.

The Christian view of bodies—that is, God's view of bodies—cannot be abstracted from the biblical account of creation. God created people with bodies, and God declared that they were good. It is sometimes hard for us modern-day Christians to grasp that central fact. Bodies are not simply pieces of furniture to decorate or display; they are not trappings about which we have conflicted feelings ("body images" that we need to revamp or retool); they are not objects to be dieted away, made to conform to popular standards, or made to perform unthinkable athletic feats with the help of drugs; they are neither tools for

scoring points nor burdens to be overcome. They are simply
good. A second-century Syrian Christian text, "The Odes of
Solomon," can remind us of this basic truth. The speaker in
the poem is God, and He is talking about human beings:

> I fashioned their members, and my own breasts I prepared
>   for them,
> That they might drink my holy milk and live by it.
> I am pleased by them,
> And am not ashamed by them.
> For my workmanship are they,
> And the strength of my thoughts.

God's creation, including human bodies, is good, but it does
not follow that everything bodies do is good. The next act of
the Christian story is the fall—Adam and Eve disobey God and
a great gulf grows between them and Him, a gulf signified by
their being pushed out of the Garden. Indeed, it is interesting
to note that sin entered the world through the bodily act of
eating, and the consequences of the fall were telegraphed on
human bodies—Adam would toil in physical labor, Eve would
feel pain in childbirth and would desire her husband (a desire
that can be understood as physical, emotional, and spiritual),
and both would die. Still, it would be an error to conclude that
in a fallen world, everything bodies do is bad. Sexual desire
is not, in itself, a wicked thing. Rather, in the fall, our sexual
desires were disordered, and one task of Christian ethics is to
help us rightly order them.

Genesis is only the starting point for understanding God's
vision of the body. Early Christians were keenly aware that, in
the phrase of church historian Wayne Meeks, "the body and
its relationships were the arena in which the moral contest of
life must take place," and the early church inaugurated a long
tradition of pondering, pontificating about, and disagreeing
over the body. The early church broke with the idea, popular
since the days of ancient Greece, that the body, and all matter,
were evil, and only the soul was good and pure and true. Today

we would call that idea *Gnosticism*, after the ancient sectar-
ian gnostics who elaborated pantheistic spiritual teachings
through the fifth century—teachings that the church deemed
heretical.

Gnostic strains run all through church history: it is easy
to find early church fathers, or Reformers, or Puritan divines
saying something that denigrates and bemoans corporeality.
(One example: Ambrose, bishop of Milan, described the body
as the "tattered garment" of the soul. He said that lifelong
celibacy is the only thing "that separates us from the beasts.")
But if the church has been dogged by a persistent Gnosticism,
it is nonetheless the case that orthodox Christianity does not
deride the body as evil. The early church set about hammering
out an alternative anthropology of human bodies, one that
understood that bodies are powerful and sometimes dangerous, but also good, worthy of honor and respect. Bodies are
something to care for and to give thanks for, not something
to revile or grudgingly accomodate. Christians do not, like
Hindus, aspire to an eternity in which we have finally escaped
our troubling bodies. Rather, we look for a hereafter in which
our bodies are resurrected and glorified.

As early as the first century, Christians worried about the
overwhelming degree to which bodies shape every aspect of our
lives. Bodies drag you down with illness; they require constant
feeding; bodily demands for rest dictate how many hours one
can spend in prayer or at work or with one's family. And then
there is the vexing matter of bodily desire. Even the noblest
and most righteous of people risk being overtaken by a desire
for sex or sleep or food.

The most important—and also perhaps the most complex—
figure in the articulation of a distinctively Christian understanding of the body is the apostle Paul. In his New Testament
epistles, Paul meditates at length upon bodies. Paul is concerned
with human bodies—what they are made of, what they are
good for, and how Christians should inhabit them. He also uses
the body as a theological metaphor that captures the essence
of the Pauline understanding of the gospel. As Anglican theo-

logian John A. T. Robinson eloquently put it, "The concept
of the body forms the keystone of Paul's theology. . . . It is from
the body of sin and death that we are delivered; it is through
the body of Christ on the Cross that we are saved; it is into His
body the Church that we are incorporated; it is by His body in
the Eucharist that this Community is sustained; it is in our body
that its new life is to be manifested; it is to a resurrection of this
body to the likeness of His glorious body that we are destined."
As Robinson notes, Paul encompasses almost all of the basics
of Christian theology—humanity, sin, incarnation, atonement,
ecclesiology, sacramentality, eschatology—in the single image
of the body.

Paul assumes that his readers value and care for their own
physical bodies. Indeed, when trying to explain to the Ephesians how much Christ loves the church, Paul draws an analogy
between Christ's love and each person's love for his own body:
"No one ever hated his own body; on the contrary, he keeps it
nourished and warm, and that is how Christ treats the church,
because it is his body, of which we are living parts." Paul takes
for granted that bodies are good things, to be nourished and
loved. He assumes his readers share his perspective and can
begin to see that Christ tends to them just as carefully as they
tend to their own bodies.

But Paul does not assume that bodies are morally neutral. He
understands that bodies are the sites of longings and temptations, of desires that can sometimes trump reason and rectitude,
of powers and passions that can be glorious but can also be
dangerous. Bodies, Paul knows, are complicated. Though they
were created good, their parts and impulses, their desires and
leanings were corrupted in the fall, just as human emotions
and human intellect were corrupted. It is hard for us moderns
to hold Paul's two truths in tension. We want things to be
clear-cut, yes or no, either/or. Bodies can be exploited; they
can be destructive and dangerous. At the same time, bodies
are good, as all of God's creation is good; and rightly ordered
by a Christian moral vision, bodies are tools God uses for His
glory. Meeks has captured the nuances of Paul's take on bod-

ies. In Meeks's phrase, Paul insists that "what is done 'in the body' is morally significant"; however, Paul also maintains that "the human predicament is the result not of the limitations of physical existence, but of sin."

Bodies are central to the Christian story. Creation inaugurates bodies that are good, but the consequences of the fall are written on our bodies—our bodies will sweat as we labor in the fields, our bodies will hurt as we bear children, and, most centrally, our bodies will die. If the fall is written on the body, salvation happens in the body too. The kingdom of God is transmitted through Jesus's body and is sustained in Christ's Body, the church. Through the bodily suffering of Christ on the cross and the bodily resurrection of Christ from the dead, we are saved. Bodies are not just mirrors in which we see the consequence of the fall; they are also, in one theologian's phrase, "where God has chosen to find us in our fallenness." Bodies are who we are and where we live; they are not just things God created us with, but means of knowing Him and abiding with Him.

Sex in Scripture

Just as scripture's vision of bodies begins in Genesis, scripture's story about sex also begins in Genesis. God's vision for humanity is established in the Garden of Eden, and the uniqueness and one-ness of the marriage relationship between Adam and Eve is inaugurated in Genesis 1–2. In the first chapters of Genesis, we learn that God created a relationship between Adam and Eve. This relationship is the context in which sex is first understood. In a graphic speech, Adam speaks of his and Eve's becoming one flesh. One-fleshness both is and is not metaphor. It captures an all-encompassing, overarching oneness—when they marry, husband and wife enter an institution that points them toward familial, domestic, emotional, and spiritual unity. But the one flesh of which Adam speaks is also overtly sexual, suggesting sexual intercourse, the only physical state other than pregnancy where it is hard to tell where one person's body stops and the other's starts.

This is why it is hard to discuss Christian sexual ethics abstracted from Christian social and marital ethics. When it comes to sex, one cannot leave out marriage. The *no* to sex outside marriage seems arbitrary and cruel apart from the Creator's *yes* to sex within marriage. Indeed, one can say that in Christianity's vocabulary the only real sex is the sex that happens in a marriage; the faux sex that goes on outside marriage is not really sex at all. The physical coming together that happens between two people who are not married is only a distorted imitation of sex, as Walt Disney's Wilderness Lodge Resort is only a simulation of real wilderness. The danger is that when we spend too much time in the simulations, we lose the capacity to distinguish between the ersatz and the real.

Even though we are fallen, we remain part of God's original creation. We were created in particular ways, with particular longings and desires and impulses. Those desires have become distorted in the fall, but they are still here within us, shaping our wants and our actions and our thoughts and our wishes. This is nowhere clearer than in human sexuality. The impulse for relationship with which God created humanity animates us—and powerful sexual desire is still with us, too. But one has only to flip through the pages of *Men's Health* or even glance at the nightly news to see that in contemporary society, men and women express sexual longings in all sorts of ways that are out of sync with God's vision of marital sex.

The Bible has something to say about all of this. The Bible understands what happened in the fall; and all the laws that biblical writers, from Moses to Paul, articulate are efforts to protect and perpetuate the ordering of things that was established in the Garden of Eden. The Mosaic laws about family relationships and sexual practices—even the faintly embarrassing and seemingly self-evident rules about avoiding incest and bestiality—do protective work, pointing to, guarding, and returning God's people to the created order, the world as God meant it to be. (Song of Songs, the erotic love poem found in Hebrew scripture, is the perfect expression of what this sexuality, restored by law and grace, looks like. It features a lover proclaiming to his beloved, "You are stately as a palm tree, and your breasts are like its clusters. . . . I will climb the palm tree and lay hold of its branches." The beloved responds with an invitation to "go out . . . into the vineyards, and see whether the vines have budded.")

Paul, in his often-quoted words about sexual behavior, is doing the same work as Mosaic law. He is thinking about sexuality in the context of the order of creation. In other words, Paul may be tweaking the specifics of Mosaic law, but in the grand scheme, he is not innovating. He is, like the leaders of the Old Testament, articulating boundaries and regulations that protect God's original intent that sex be expressed in marriage.

What are the specifics of Paul's vision for human sexuality? The main category of sexual behavior that Paul wants Christians in his care (by which I mean the first-century Christians who received his epistles, and also the twenty-first-century Christians who read his letters as sacred scripture today) to avoid is, in New Testament Greek, *porneia*. This term crops up fifty-five times in the New Testament. It is translated alternatively as fornication, lust, and sexual immorality; one dictionary of New Testament Greek defines *porneia* as "illicit sexual intercourse in general," another as "sexual immorality of any kind, often with the implication of prostitution." Just as the general category of dishonesty encompasses lying, embezzlement, and clever deception by omission, *porneia* is a capacious category of sexual impropriety that encompasses many different sexual deeds. *Porneia* seems to include, among other sexual misdeeds, prostitution (the Greek word for prostitute was *porne*, etymologically related to *porneia*, both of which are the root of the English word *pornography*). Matthew 5:32 and 19:9 indicate that *porneia* includes adultery. And the context of 1 Corinthians 5, in which Paul forbids a man to have sex with his father's wife, suggests that *porneia* includes incest.

The sixth and seventh chapter of Paul's first epistle to the Corinthians show both how broad and how specific the category of *porneia* is. In 1 Corinthians 6, Paul invokes *porneia* when he is forbidding Corinthians from patronizing prostitutes. In the next chapter, Paul uses *porneia* again, this time telling the unmarried and the widows that it is better to marry than to burn with desire. In this second passage, logic tells us that *porneia* must mean sex outside of marriage—if the only two options are marriage or smoldering with desire, it follows that sex outside of marriage is not an option. And, according to Paul, this sin is no minor peccadillo. As Lewis Smedes summarizes, "If unmarried sexual intercourse was wrong, it was a serious wrong; it ought not even be talked about (Eph. 5:3). God's will is that we abstain from fornication, not giving way to 'the passion of lust like heathen who do not know God' (1 Thess. 4:6). *[Porneia]* is sin; intercourse by unmarried people is *[porneia]*, therefore intercourse by unmarried people is sin."

Paul sometimes gets a reputation as a killjoy, a first-century prude who's concerned above all else with regulating people's sexual behavior. Abstracted from his larger vision of helping people live into God's ideals for creation, Paul's vision of human sexuality does indeed seem like a list of arbitrary rules. But Paul is not writing in a vacuum. He uses the literary technique of repetition to direct the reader's attention back to Genesis. In the middle of his first letter to the Corinthians, right after enjoining the Corinthians not to sleep with prostitutes and right before instructing the unmarried that it is better to marry than to burn, Paul quotes Genesis 2:24: "The two shall become one flesh." Paul's quotation is something of shorthand—it tells the reader to flip back to the second chapter of Genesis to find both the basis for and the elaboration of Paul's words on sexuality.

One could play clever philological games with these passages in Paul, insisting that even dictionary-writers don't know exactly what *porneia* means; maybe it doesn't mean premarital sex at all. Let us set aside the fact that in 1 Corinthians 7 it is hard to read *porneia* as anything other than sex outside of marriage. The point is not to endlessly parse Paul's particular phrasing in any one extract from his epistles. It does not, in the end, matter very much that the dictionary-writers disagree about the details of New Testament Greek. Scripture gives us a context for reading the rest of scripture, and what we learn about God's vision for sexuality in Genesis shapes how we understand words about sexuality in the rest of the Bible. Paul understands sex as part of the ordering of creation. Paul's words cannot be unhinged from his larger vision of the world, a vision set out at the beginning of scripture.

This is not just a lesson in reading. It is also a pastoral point. Consider, as an example, the recent experience of my friend Kara, a campus minister in Illinois. Recently a student came to her, on fire for the Lord, and said, "I want to follow and serve Jesus, and the one thing I really want to know is, how far can I go with my boyfriend?" One could, I suppose, answer that question simply by pointing to a few verses from Paul, but a more complete, and perhaps more compelling, instruction is to begin with the picture of intended reality that is laid out in Genesis. Kara realized that answering her student's question required first answering a host of larger questions: *Who created us, and for what ends? What is God's creational intent?* and *What are we made for?*

I'll hazard a guess about Kara's student. When she's sitting on the sofa in a dark den with her boyfriend, random verses from Paul may not do much work. However, if this student's community helps form in her an understanding that she is God's creature, made for God's best purposes, she may indeed think very differently—even righteously—about sex, and bodies, and the context in which those bodies are to touch and be touched.

Our bodies and how we inhabit them point to the order of creation. God made us for sex within marriage; this is what the Reformed tradition would call a creational law. To see the biblical witness as an attempt to direct us to the created order, to God's rule of creation, is not to appeal to self-interest in a therapeutic or false way. It is rather to recognize the true goodness of God's creation; things as they were in the Garden of Eden are things at their most nourishing, they are things as they are meant to be. This is what Paul is saying when he speaks to the Corinthians: *Don't you know that when you give your body to a prostitute, you are uniting yourself to her?* To ask that question is to speak the wisdom of Proverbs in the idiom of law. It is a law that invites us into the created order of marital sex; a law that rightly orders our created desires for sexual pleasure and sexual connectedness; a law, in short, that cares for us and protects us, written by a Lawgiver who understands that life outside of God's created intent destroys us. By contrast, life lived inside the contours of God's law humanizes us and makes us beautiful. It makes us creatures living well in the created order. It gives us the opportunity to become who we are meant to be.

3

COMMUNAL SEX

*Or, Why Your Neighbor Has Any Business Asking You
What You Did Last Night*

Salvation in Christ is being adopted (baptism), made members
of a people, Israel, and the church. We really believe that if we
were not part of this people we could not be saved. So when
the church has opinions about how you spend your money,
how you have sex, how you vote, this is salvation. You are not
simply being saved from personal greed or licentiousness, you
are thereby being made a member of God's people.

—William Willimon and Stanley Hauerwas

One of my favorite novelists is Barbara Pym. Pym, who was
born in Shropshire in 1913, wrote novels set in post-war English villages populated by vicars, spinsters, and well-meaning
but slightly inept housewives. Pym was a master of the comedy
of manners, simultaneously arch and generous, and she is often
likened to Jane Austen.

Her third novel, *Jane and Prudence*, depicts the long-standing friendship of Jane, a middle-aged minister's wife adjusting to small-town life in a new rural vicarage, and her erstwhile student Prudence, an office worker in London. Twenty-nine-year-old Prudence is rapidly on her way to old-maid status, and Jane attempts to fix her up with the recently widowed Fabian Driver. Prudence condescends to go on a few dates with Fabian, but doesn't reward Jane with any juicy details of their assignations.

One week, Jane pays Prudence a visit in London. Jane is alarmed when her friend answers the door clad in "a long garment of dark red velvet, a sort of rather grand dressing-gown." The vermilion gown is "not the sort of garment a vicar's wife could be said to possess." It stands in dramatic contrast to Jane's own worn camel-hair robe. "Had she entertained Fabian in her red velvet dressing-gown?" Jane wonders, shocked. Sipping a cup of Ovaltine, she endeavors to learn just how intimate Prudence's relationship with Fabian Driver has become.

"Does Fabian like you in red?" she asked bluntly.

"Yes. I think so," said Prudence rather vaguely.

"Has he seen you in that?"

"I can't remember really—he probably has."

"I suppose it's all right in London," said Jane, thoughtfully stirring her Ovaltine.

"How do you mean?"

"Well, to entertain a man in one's dressing-gown."

"It isn't a dressing-gown," said Prudence rather impatiently; "it's a housecoat. And in any case I don't know what you mean by 'all right'."

"No, it's a very decent garment really, with long sleeves and a high neck." Jane picked up a fold of the full skirt and stroked the velvet. "I suppose what I meant was would people think anything of it if they knew."

Prudence laughed. "Oh, really, Jane! It certainly isn't like you to worry about what other people would think."

"No. I suppose it isn't. I was just thinking of you, really. A married woman does feel in some way responsible for her unmarried friends, you know."

"Really? That hadn't occurred to me. In any case, I'm perfectly well able to look after myself," said Prudence rather touchily.

"Darling, of course! I only wondered . . ." Jane paused, for really it was difficult to know how to ask what she wanted to know, assuming that she had any right to ask such a question. "I suppose everything is all right between you and Fabian?" she began tentatively.

"All right? Why, yes."

"I mean, there's nothing *wrong* between you," Jane laboured, using an expression she had sometimes seen in the cheaper women's papers where girls asked how they should behave when their boy-friends wanted them to "do wrong."

"But I don't understand you, Jane. Did you think we'd quarrelled or something? Because we certainly haven't, I can assure you."

"No, it wasn't that. I don't seem to be putting it very clearly, what I was trying to ask was, are you Fabian's *mistress*?" As soon as she had said it, Jane found herself wanting to laugh. It was such a ridiculous word; it reminded her of full-blown Restoration comedy women . . . or Edwardian ladies kept in pretty little houses with wrought-iron balconies. . . .

Prudence burst into laughter, in which Jane was able to join her with some relief.

"Really, Jane, what an extraordinary question—you *are* a funny old thing! Am I Fabian's *mistress*? Is there anything *wrong* between us? I couldn't imagine what you meant!"

Jane looked up from her Ovaltine hopefully. "I don't really know how people behave these days," she said.

"Well, I mean to say—one just doesn't ask," Prudence went on. "Surely either one is or one isn't and there's no need to ask coy questions about it. Now, Jane, what about a hot-water bottle? . . ." Prudence stood up, slim and elegant in her red velvet housecoat.

Jane said, ". . . I don't mind about a bottle, really I don't, though if you have a spare one it might be a comfort." She felt a little peevish, as if she had been cheated, as indeed she had.

She also felt a little foolish—naturally, she should have known
that Prudence was (or wasn't) Fabian's mistress.

Though written over fifty years ago, in a perhaps more delicate and decorous age, this scene perfectly demonstrates the
discomfort of conversation between friends about sex. Jane,
surely, is curious, and perhaps she is even living vicariously
through Prudence, but she is above all trying to care for her
friend. Yet she is unsure how exactly to do so. She worries
that she might be out of line inquiring about Prudence's sexual
behavior. Lacking the words for her concern, she resorts to
awkward quotations from women's magazines. All in all, her
attempt to talk to Prudence about her relationship with Fabian
is a dismal failure. Jane feels as though she's been cheated,
because, in fact, Prudence evades her questions and tells her
nothing. For her part, Prudence thinks Jane, with her whole-
some chocolate beverage, is a bit of a bore. Prudence is a
liberated gal—she doesn't care what anyone thinks about her.
Though Prudence has invited Jane into her home, she can't
ultimately invite her into her life, and instead sends Jane off
to bed like a child.

"The affair was none of their business"

Most of us, on some level, share Prudence's assumptions.
It is not surprising that Prudence is miffed—does Jane really
have a right to chide her about her romance with Fabian? And
Jane's confusion is certainly understandable. Aren't our friends'
private lives . . . private? We ought not risk looking prudish, or
invasive, or presumptuous, by putting our oar in. In Prudence's
phrase, either one is or one isn't, and one just doesn't ask.

In contemporary society, sex is public—moms go on talk
shows and confess to sleeping with their daughters' boyfriends,
Calvin Klein models expose their body parts in magazine ads.
But if sex is public, it is not communal. Americans consider
sex a fine topic of public disclosure but we insist that sex is

also private, nobody's business but mine and the person with whom I'm doing it. I can show you my midriff in public, and I can make out with my boyfriend on a park bench, but there is no communal grammar that allows you to talk to me about this body I am exposing in front of you.

Underpinning everything else we say about sex is the assumption and insistence that you ought to keep your nose out of my bedroom. Supreme Court Justice John Harry Blackmun, dissenting from the 1986 decision *Bowers v. Hardwick*, declared that "how a person engages in sex should be irrelevant as a matter of state law. Sexual intimacy is a sensitive, key relationship of human existence and the development of human personality. In a diverse nation such as ours, we must preserve the individual freedom to choose, and not imply that there are any 'right' ways of conducting relationships."

Variations on that theme pervade our popular culture. From movies and TV shows to online mags and the nightly news, everyone is telling us that sex is private. As Elliot Garfield says in the 1970s film *The Goodbye Girl*, "If I do attempt to have carnal knowledge of that gorgeous bod that'll be her option, my problem, and none of your business." Even the satirical Simpsons reiterate the point. In an episode tellingly called "Secrets of a Successful Marriage," Homer and Marge attend a marriage seminar. Homer tells the tale of an anonymous couple—Mr. X and Mrs. Y—who practice the delicate art of elbow nibbling underneath the covers. But Homer blows X and Y's cover when he blurts out, "So anyway, Mr. X would say, 'Marge, if this doesn't get your motor running, my name isn't Homer J. Simpson.'" Marge, furious that Homer has shared something about their bedroom behavior with the seminar, kicks him out of the house.

I was surprised to find the same theme sounded in Danielle Crittenden's recent novel *Amanda Bright @ Home*. Crittenden, who has made a name for herself bashing second-wave feminism and the sexual revolution, is very much a cultural conservative, and *Amanda Bright @ Home*, on the whole, valorizes a pretty traditional and conservative view of things.

No swingingly single heroine here. Rather, our Amanda is a smart and sassy Ivy League grad who has turned her back on money and professional glamour to stay at home with her kids. She's a little ambivalent about her choice, but she ultimately finds fulfillment at home with her three little ones. Most women will close the novel thinking they should marry, have lots of babies, and then devote themselves to the arts of housewifery and childcare. Yet the notion that sex is private has captivated even the folks who live in Amanda's homey and traditional world. One night Amanda's best friend, Susie, comes for dinner, new boyfriend in tow. Amanda is charmed by the beau, but just before dessert, Susie tells Amanda that he's married. Amanda, shocked and angry, is worried about her friend. Amanda's husband, Bob, pooh-poohs her concern, insisting that Susie is a grown-up and her affairs are, well, her affairs. Amanda finds herself persuaded by Bob's reasoning: "Bob's words had been reasonable enough. Susie *was* a big girl, the affair was none of their business." Susie was a grown woman, Amanda reasons, a free agent, and even her best friend really has no place questioning Susie's choice to sleep with someone else's husband.

Amanda's monologue neatly summarizes our society's most basic message about sex: one person's sexual behavior is not anyone else's concern. And if your best friend doesn't have permission to voice her worry when you commit adultery— with both its blatant violation of the Ten Commandments and its obvious capacity to hurt other people and wreak social havoc—certainly no one has permission to utter a word about a little thing like premarital sex.

Put simply, this is a lie. And it is a fairly new lie. For most of human history, people of many different cultures have agreed that societies must order certain forms of exchange in order to survive. Communities have ordered language, establishing grammars and vocabularies that shape how people communicate with one another; they have ordered the exchange of money, property, and labor; and they have ordered the practice of sex. As essayist, poet, and novelist Wendell Berry has put it, "Sex, like any other necessary, precious, and volatile power that is commonly held, is everybody's business."

In the last half-century, however, that assumption has been routed, replaced by the axioms of individualism and autonomy. Indeed, today the idea that sex "is everybody's business" sounds alternately shocking and silly. Instead, we are more prone to think like my friend Roxanne, who chuckles and says, "Look, we're two consenting adults. Why is what we do under the sheets anyone else's concern?"

There are, of course, some practical answers to Roxanne's question, not least that her sex is my business because sex can lead to babies, and the society that Roxanne and I share has a vested interest in defining and maintaining the family structures that care for babies.

But Roxanne and her boyfriend use condoms, so it is easy for her to dismiss any concern I might have about kids. Today, thanks to the Pill, we can generally (if not completely) sever the connection between sex and child-making; indeed, the advent of reliable birth control was a major factor in privatizing sex in the West. "I'm not going to burden society with an unexpected and unwanted child," says Roxanne, "so I'm free to do what I want, right? Or what about my mom? She didn't get remarried after Dad died, but she's well past menopause. She won't be conceiving any babies, so she and her gentleman friend can surely make their own decisions about what they do in bed."

To be honest, I appreciate Roxanne's rejection of my practical and pragmatic suggestion that sex is communal because babies are communal. Procreation ought not be severed from sexual conversation (we will return to procreation in the next chapter); but arguing that sex is "everybody's business" only because everybody is interested in preserving stable families in which children can be reared is on some level a practical argument, and practical arguments are, finally, unsatisfying, because they don't get at the core of what's at stake.

It is sometimes hard for me to talk to Roxanne about sex because she and I don't share some basic assumptions. For starters, the way I talk about sex is conditioned by the beginning of Genesis. The understanding (laid out in chapter two) that sex is made for marriage is vital to my belief that sex is a communal task. Marriage serves as the biblical analogy par excellence to the relationship between God and His people. Over and over in sacred scripture, that relationship is described as a marriage. When the people of Israel are faithful to God, Israel is described as a bride; when she turns away from God, she is called a harlot. Similarly, the writers of the New Testament found that one way to capture the relationship between Christ and the church was to draw an analogy to husband and wife. Through these analogies, marriage is substantively linked to community. Marriage—because of what marriage is, the analogue to God and His relationship to His people—precedes sex. This ordering of marriage and sex—the understanding that marriage contains sex, rather than that sex adorns marriage—implies a resonance between sex and community.

But perhaps a more important disagreement between Roxanne and me has to do with individualism. The actors in Roxanne's question are "two consenting adults," unmoored from any community or society, free to make their own decisions. So long as they don't violate the other's consent, they can do as they please.

Even on Roxanne's individualistic terms, terms keyed to a world where everyone is a free agent, sex can be rightly understood as a matter of communal concern. Sex is communal because it is real. Sex has consequences. Sex is dangerous and delightful and tempestuous and elemental, and it matters. What we do with our bodies, what we do sexually, shapes our persons. How we comport ourselves sexually shapes who we are. If we believe that sex forms us, then it goes without saying that it is public business, because how we build the persons we are—persons who are social and communal and political and economic beings—is itself a matter of social concern.

Even in America, which sometimes seems to value individualism above all else, we never hesitate to insist that formative institutions are public business. We readily agree, for example, that education is a matter of concern for all members of our community, even those citizens who don't have school-age kids—because we understand that education forms the children who grow up to be the adult citizens that constitute our community. We have heated debates about controversial exhibits at art museums, because we recognize that the art we spend time with shapes the persons we are, and who we are is a public problem. As with art and education, so with sex. Because sex forms us, sex is a community matter. Sexual ethics make good sense even in a world governed by individualism.

Still, the real place of disagreement between Roxanne and me is the assumption of individualism itself. In a world where the basic unit of ethical meaning is the individual, Roxanne's stance carries real weight. But in the Christian universe, the individual is *not* the vital unit of ethical meaning. For Christians, the most basic images, metaphors, and signs are corporate, and the basic unit of ethical meaning is the Body, the community. Israel experiences covenantal fidelity as a people, and the People of God is a collective—not merely an aggregate of individual persons, each doing his or her own thing, but a body. In the Bible, God elects the People of Israel as a body. He sustains them as a body. And, finally, He redeems them as a body.

This talk about community is not mere metaphorizing. The community has a role in making ethics. Paul makes this clear when he instructs the Galatians to hold one another accountable for sin: "Brothers, if someone is caught in a sin, you who are spiritual should restore him gently. But watch yourself, or you also may be tempted. Carry each other's burdens, and in this way you will fulfill the law of Christ."

That passage in Galatians, if we construe it uncharitably, can lead us to envision a community that functions primarily as a police force: Christians' responsibilities to one another begin and end with peering into other Christians' bedroom windows and sounding the alarm if something illicit is going on.

While one task of any community is to enforce its own codes when they are being violated, perhaps the prior task of the community is to make sense of the ethical codes that are being enforced. Here the community is not so much cop as storyteller, telling and retelling the foundational stories of the community itself, sustaining the stories that make sense of the community's norms. This storytelling is part of the working out of God's grace in the church. We, the church, retell our own story—we do this every time we read scripture, every time we celebrate the Lord's Supper, and (hopefully) every time we minister to one another. And that retelling is part of what enables us to live into the story. It is the community that ensures that ethics is not about the dispensing of cut-and-dried answers to moral questions, but that ethics is a story with meaning and power.

Sociologist James Hunter gets at this point in his study *A Death of Character*. Character—the making and sustaining of character—is a communal event, not an individual possession. Contra the psychologists, who would say that character accrues autonomously in individual people, Hunter shows that character is a social thing. Far from innate and purely natural, character is formed and learned in societies, and when the social prerequisites for character formation disappear, no amount of individual striving will culminate in character. "The story implicit within the word 'character,'" writes Hunter, "is one that is shared. It is never just for the isolated individual. The narrative integrates the self within communal purposes, binding dissimilar others to common ends. Character outside of a lived community, the entanglements of complex social relationships, and their shared story, is impossible."

Christians have to work hard to overcome the pervasive message that my sexual behavior is none of your business. Though we are willing to talk about sex from the pulpit, we are often less comfortable initiating hard conversations with our brothers and sisters about sex in people's real, day-to-day lives. The Christian community senses that sex is a matter of communal concern, but we are hard-pressed to articulate exactly why. We have understandably absorbed the story our surrounding culture so forcefully tells us, trading our vision of community for American notions of individuals and free agents.

A story that my friend Carrie shared with me may illustrate. Carrie was two years out of college, living in Minneapolis in a funky, rambling Victorian with six other Christian women. Her boyfriend, Thad, lived down the block. Carrie and Thad were not having sex, but they were doing everything but having sex, including spending the night with each other regularly. And of course none of Carrie's roommates knew for sure that they weren't having sex—all they knew was that Carrie and Thad spent a lot of nighttime hours together in his apartment. But not one of Carrie's roomies ever asked her a single question about what was going on behind closed doors. No one ever posed a loving inquiry, or a gentle rebuke, or even an oblique offer of an ear. Probably Carrie and Thad's friends were simply made uncomfortable by the prospect of raising the tough issues of sex and chastity. They probably did not want to intrude, or seem nosy.

But the Bible tells us to intrude—or rather, the Bible tells us that talking to one another about what is really going on in our lives is in fact not an intrusion at all, because what's going on in my life is already your concern; by dint of the baptism that made me your sister, my joys are your joys and my crises are your crises. We are called to speak to one another lovingly, to be sure, and with edifying, rather than gossipy or hurtful, goals. But we are called nonetheless to transform seemingly private matters into communal matters. Of course, premarital sexual behavior is just one of many instances of this larger point. Christians also need to speak courageously and transparently, for example, about the seemingly private matters of Christian marriage—there would be, I suspect, a lot fewer divorces in the church if married Christians exposed their domestic lives, their fights and tensions and squabbles, to loving wisdom, advice, and sometimes rebuke from their community. Christians might claim less credit-card debt if small-group members shared their bank account statements with one another. I suspect that if my best friend had permission to scrutinize my Day-timer, I would inhabit time better. Speaking to one another about our sexual selves is just one (admittedly risky) instance of a larger piece of Christian discipleship: being community with each other.

Household Sex

Wendell Berry provides us a good starting point for thinking about sex and community. Berry's account of sexual ethics—his critique of modern sexuality and his vision of a more appropriate and redemptive sexual practice—rests on the rails of his larger account of the deterioration of modern society. Berry believes that modern life is bedeviled by the veneration of autonomy. We moderns conceive of ourselves as disparate, self-sufficient, and isolated atoms. Whether we realize it or not, our highest pursuits—in science, in politics, in personal happiness, in culture, in morality, and, at times, in religious life—function to maximize a sense of our own distinctiveness. We calibrate career success in terms of how well our jobs attend to our specific desires. We even conceive of America's great democracy as a way to get our own interests heard, rather than a way to achieve or articulate larger social goods. And on it goes. At each turn, modern society glorifies achievements of independence and specificity, reveling in the way human beings are able seemingly to shrug off their natural dependencies.

It is not surprising that this modern refusal to acknowledge the way humans are dependent creatures—on their surroundings, on each other, on forces beyond their control, on God—should manifest itself in sexual terms. We create rarified and unearthly standards of beauty, and evaluate the sexual attractiveness of both ourselves and other people by the degree to which they resemble those standards. We often conceive of sex as an athletic exercise, which when done well is about dexterity, technique, and endurance. Pick up any women's or men's magazine, and read the advice columns and the advertisements: our contemporary culture tells us that sex is little more than recreation. All in all, sex has been denatured, dismembered, and desacralized.

The point is not to offer yet another flat-footed religious critique of secular degradations. What appears to be a critique of modernity is also a critique of religious life in modernity. A robust yet judicious understanding of the communal nature of sexual behavior requires that Christians enact both a thicker understanding of sex and a thicker understanding of community. To return sex to its proper place within creation, to revivify a gracious and salutary sexual existence, we need to root out modern and hyperindividualistic notions about sex, and come to understand the place of sex in the Christian—and human—community.

The insidious individualistic notions that turn sex into no more than entertainment not only shape how Americans think about illicit activities like premarital sex; they even infiltrate and affect how we think about marital sex. Husband and wife, too, judge their sexual life by aesthetic norms. Spouses have come to view marital sex as principally a way for an individual husband and an individual wife to get individual needs met.

Enter Wendell Berry, who suggests that marital sex ought not be an individual project at all. In a rich domestic context, sex is not about individual desires that happen to be neatly matched, but is rather an embodied way of entering into community with one's spouse and of enacting God's love.

At the heart of Berry's vision is an idea called the household. *Household* seems, at first blush, to be just a synonym for *home*, but it is actually quite different from what most of us mean when we speak of home.

Today some of us think of homes as warm places where people come together for affection and love. Others think of homes as sites of dysfunction, places that should have been filled with warmth but were instead marked by neglect and abuse. And some of us reside not in homes but in houses—physical dwelling places where people who happen to be related to one another (or who happen to be roommates) live out their relatively separate lives. Each family member has his own TV, his own cell phone, his own car. We each have our own busy schedules that often preclude our eating breakfast or dinner together. We go to our houses to refuel and rest our bodies, and then we return to the places that really matter—our schools, our businesses, the places where we earn the money to pay for all those cell phones and cars.

A household, by contrast, is a place of shared mission, of shared work. Think back to the eighteenth century when people did most of their productive labor together, in family units, in their households. Mothers and daughters spun flax together. Children helped parents plant and harvest crops. I don't mean to romanticize the difficulties and privations of life in earlier centuries—work was hard, medical care was sketchy, life was short.

And yet there was something powerfully good about those earlier households, something missing from many of our homes and houses today. There was a togetherness born not merely of affection but of mutual work. It didn't really matter if you liked your husband on a given Tuesday. You were stuck working with him all day anyhow. Your togetherness, your relationship, didn't rely on the caprice of your feelings. You were bound together, primarily, by a common undertaking—making your productive household run. Your household was not a place where individuals happened to congregate; it was a place of genuine mutuality.

To understand the good work that work does for families and neighbors, think about backyard cookouts. Sure, ordering pizza from Domino's would be simpler, and less labor-intensive than stoking up the grill, chopping all that cabbage for coleslaw, tending to the hamburgers and hot dogs, making sure they don't get overcooked—but when I work together with my neighbors, even simple work like cabbage-chopping, I am participating in a shared enterprise with them, and that sharing strengthens the ties of our relationship. So you don't have to be an eighteenth-century farmer to begin to conceive of your home as a household. Rather, beginning to approach your meals, chores, and furnishings as part of a rich domestic economy, opportunities to connect you, your family, and your neighbors in truly shared undertakings.

In an essay called "The Body and the Earth," Berry urges married couples to integrate their sexual lives into the larger,

holistic project of creating a household. Indeed, Berry is concerned not only with what happens in individual households,
but with the ways households, families, and marriages are part
of larger neighborhoods and communities. Berry wants us
to envision domestic life and sex, marriage and the marriage
bed, as "a more generous enclosure—a household welcoming
to neighbors and friends." We should view all of society as a
series of concentric circles—households sit at the center, and
they are encircled by neighborhoods, and neighborhoods are
encircled by communities, and communities by towns, civic
bodies, whole societies. (Or perhaps the more appropriate
metaphor is the wedding cake. At the very top are a bride and
groom, and they are supported by a layer of household, a layer
of family, and a final layer of community and society.)

Marriages, in other words, are not meant to be simply pairs
of people in love; they are institutions out of which cultures
and societies are formed. Households are the foundations of
communities. Because marriage *is* a community, marital sex is
rightly understood as the glue that binds "a woman and a man
not only to each other, but to the community of marriage, the
amorous communion at which all couples sit." In productive
households, married sex can be "a communion of workmates,"
not a romanticized "lover's paradise," nor a "kind of marketplace in which husband and wife represent each other as sexual
property." And marital sex should, in Berry's phrase, "empower
and . . . grace" the household and the community.

Berry claims that "the disintegration of community" began
when we started treating marital sex as a wholly private matter, when we severed the connections that link marriages to
households and neighborhoods and communities. The history
of dance, Berry says, is illustrative: in the seventeenth and
eighteenth centuries, "the old ring dances, in which all couples
danced together," were gradually replaced by "social ballroom
dancing, in which each couple dances alone." For many people
today, of course, social ballroom dancing is a thing of the past.
It has been replaced by the rave, in which a crowd of people

dance not so much as a community, but as a group of individuals, boogying in the same room, alone.

What does all this mean, in practical terms? It is one thing for a couple to open up their household to their sexuality—to recognize that sexuality is, in Berry's phrase, a "nurturing discipline," and allow it to form and shape the work and daily life of their home. It is quite another for them to understand their sexuality as contributing to a larger community. Yet when we realize that sexual love is a primary force in constructing a household, and that households are primary components of constructing community, it begins to appear, indeed, that sexuality is something that should have a public, communal face. The question, of course, is in what way. Sexuality is an integral part of human mutual dependence. Sex, then, is a communal topic. We Christians—whose primary idioms are not individualistic, but communal, the Body of God and the church—are to see in sexuality the bonds of community.

It is an attractive vision that Berry lays out. It calls to us in our hectic, isolated lives. And yet this idea of community can rankle. The logic that links my body to sex to marriage to household to family to neighborhood to community is compelling, but it seems alien. Individualism and autonomy are so essential to the modern story that even Christians have trouble parsing the relationship between ourselves, our bodies, families, homes, and our communities. We know that bodies are not private property in the same way a car or a sweater is private property. We agree that marriage and sex are topics worthy of communal consideration, but we have trouble remembering, and knowing how to enact, all the communal and corporate language of the church.

But the resources for reiterating and inhabiting Christian community are still visible and audible in the church, not least in the marriage ceremony, which makes plain that sex is a part of the new relationship the community is promising to uphold. In Thomas Cranmer's sixteenth-century language, brides and grooms vow that "with my body, I thee worship." Not a private affair between two atomized adults who contract to live together, Christian weddings are essentially communal. The bride and groom are surrounded by their community, and one of the most important moments of the ceremony is when the minister asks the congregation whether it will do all in its power to uphold the bride and groom in their covenant of marriage. The congregation answers, "We will."

As the church, we tell the story of creation and redemption, and we speak to one another about sexuality's place in that story. We animate the story through confession and confrontation. We embroider the story with practical tips that help people manage and express desire. We live the story through a series of institutions that display redemption to the world and enable the gospel to transform God's people through sacrament, and hospitality, and prayer.

I was once asked what I would say to a friend whom I knew was having premarital sex; would I do any better than awkward, Ovaltine-sipping Jane? I told my interlocutor that the first step in speaking to my friends about sex was making sure that we enjoyed relationships built on top of hundreds of ordinary shared experiences—plays attended together and pumpkins carved together and accompanying one another on doctors appointments and changing the oil together. To say this is not to side-step the question. Community doesn't come about simply by having hard, intimate conversations. Having hard, intimate conversations is part of what is possible when people are already opening up their day-to-day lives to one another.

Sex is communal rather than private, but it is still personal rather than public. To say there are communal rights to sexual behavior is not to imagine a world where Mr. Married offers a Christianized version of locker-room chat with his buddies in the pews. It is not to imply that my married friends need to regale me with details every time they make love.

To say that sex is communal, rather, is to remind Carrie's roommates that they have not just a right but an obligation to speak to Carrie about sexual sin. It is to encourage married

Christians to speak to one another—not just about sexual *sin*, but about all the complicated emotional and physical thickets one can find oneself in when one is having sex. It is to urge Christians to speak frankly to one another about the realities of chastity, about the thrills and tediums of married sex, about the rich meanings inherent in being sexual persons who live in bodies. It is to ask the church to serve as narrator, reminding ourselves who we are, and why we do what we do.

4

STRAIGHT TALK I

Lies Our Culture Tells about Sex

Sexual delight, sexual drive, sexual instincts . . . How do we talk about such things? They arise from some place stunningly prior to sentence construction and word choice, prior to argument and persuasion. But talk about it we do, by golly, just about endlessly.

—Catherine Wallace

In May 2004, Jessica Cutler found her fifteen minutes of fame. A young staffer in Republican Senator Mike DeWine's Washington office and a relative newcomer to D.C., Cutler had begun keeping a weblog, or "blog," of her social and sexual adventures. In her online diary, she described the dates and sex she was having with six different Washingtonians, including a married Bush appointee who gave her a few hundred dollars each time they met in a hotel. (For readers who had trouble keeping up with the half-dozen lovers, Cutler helpfully included a "key to keeping my sex life straight.") Of working in the

U.S. Senate, Cutler wrote: "I could not care less about gov or politics, but . . . these marble hallways are such great places for meeting boys and showing off my outfits." Then there was a lawyer she'd sworn off because sex with him was physically uncomfortable. When he e-mailed her asking to meet up again, she replied, "From now on, we should go out drinking before we go back to your place. I think that would improve everything." One Wednesday, she had so many assignations that she summed up her day as "a revolving door of men, with me pushing one out after another."

She'd intended her blog to be read by just close friends, but it is hard to keep anything private online. After just a few steamy entries, Cutler's diary made it onto Wonkette, a gossipy talk-of-the-town website much beloved on Capitol Hill. Cutler lost her job, and each of her six lovers lost interest in her, but she was suddenly the it-girl of newspapers around the world, and she snagged a layout for *Playboy* and a lucrative contract for a chick-lit novel based on her Washington exploits.

Cutler may be, as one pundit described her, "an extreme," partaking in sexual escapades that don't represent "mainstream majority behavior." Nonetheless, she encapsulates a lot of truths about our culture. For starters, she tells us about second-wave feminism gone haywire. Feminist mamas challenged a double standard that awarded men but punished women for having sex, but Cutler and fellow travelers have taken "sexual liberation" to an extreme that would have been unthinkable to most feminist activists in the 1960s. As critic Naomi Wolf explains, "The feminist message of autonomy [has gotten] filtered through a pornographized culture. The message [young women] heard was just go for it sexually. . . . [W]e've raised a generation of young women—and men—who don't understand sexual ethics. . . . They don't see sex as sacred or even very important anymore. Sex has been commodified and drained of its deeper meaning."

Cutler also tells us something about the culture of communication. "Everyone should have a blog," she says. For blogs, like Amazon.com reader reviews, turn everyone into an author.

They give everyone a pulpit, and create the possibility that everyone can have an audience, regardless how tawdry the show. For good and for ill, blogging is one of Internet Revolution's new technologies, which sidestep traditional gatekeepers like publishers and newspaper editors. As Cutler put it, blogs are the "most democratic thing ever."

And if her adulterous quasi-prostitution may not be mainstream, the ease with which Jessica Cutler—and the media who made her a starlet—talk and write about sex certainly is. April Witt, writing about Cutler in the *Washington Post Magazine*, observed that although the frequency of Jessica's flings surprised some Washingtonians, "Jessica's frank talk about sex didn't strike [anyone] as unusual." A twenty-seven-year-old advertising executive who had never had a one-night stand said that "[Cutler] depresses me. I don't think people can do those kind of things without emotional repercussions. [Still,] women love to talk about sex. That's what we do when we get together and drink. If I was in a relationship with someone I cared about and I was concerned about my performance, I'd talk about it in graphic detail with my friends." What shocked Washingtonians was what Cutler had done in all those hotel rooms; no one was shocked that she'd talked so freely about sex.

Conversations, debates, and revelations about sex are everywhere in our common culture. There's a lot of talk about sex in Internet chatrooms, and on the airwaves, and in *Good Housekeeping*, the *New York Times*, and *GQ*. Sexual chatter is downright ambient. According to one study, over 14,000 sexual references are shown on TV per year, and the average person will view over 100,000 of those references in his or her lifetime.

It's not, in theory, a bad thing that we talk about sex. Indeed, that we can speak in public—in our families and churches and civic spaces and shopping malls—about sex is something of an improvement over the days where one was forbidden even to utter the word *sex* in polite society.

The problem is not *that* we talk about sex. The problem is *how* we talk about sex. So much of what we say about sex is wrong: deceptive, distorted, misleading. This matters, because the way we talk about sex reflects and forms the way we think about, and ultimately the way we practice, sex. Much of what we say about sex in public is, simply, false. And when we tell falsehoods about sex, and listen to falsehoods about sex, we wind up living falsehoods about sex. Herewith, an exploration of four powerful lies that pervade our sexual culture.

Lie #1: Sex Can Be Wholly Separated from Procreation

In a recent issue of *Vogue*, I saw an ad for a birth control patch. The ad assured readers that this new patch is "as effective as the Pill (99 percent when used correctly)." Women, you paste this patch on your upper arm or shoulder blade and then you can stop worrying—both about getting pregnant and about popping those pesky birth control pills every morning. The message was straightforward. Birth control: "On your body. Off your mind. . . . It's that simple."

Historians generally agree that without the advent of oral contraception the sexual revolution of the 1960s probably wouldn't have happened. In order for people, especially women, to feel free to have sex with people to whom they've no commitment, they need to be reasonably sure that pregnancy will not ensue. Birth control pills can make us about 99 percent sure. Right-wing rhetoric not withstanding, we do have the technology to prevent most unwanted pregnancies most of the time. Birth control pills and condoms aren't foolproof, but neither are they foolhardy; they are, in fact, pretty effective.

Official teaching in the Roman Catholic Church, articulated in the 1968 encyclical *Humanae Vitae*, forbids the use of "artificial contraceptives" such as condoms and birth control pills; but Protestants (and many American Catholics) have readily embraced birth control. Only recently have some Protestants, concerned about the way contraception radically severs the connection between sex and procreation, begun to rethink our unambiguous endorsement of birth control.

Christians, it seems to me, can legitimately disagree with one another about contraception. Still, if some of us opt to use contraception and others do not, we might all press some questions about the way birth control affects our understanding and practice of sexuality. In other words, Christians can accept birth control while also critically examining the culture of contraception. The question we need to ask, I think, is what kind of sexual persons contraception invites us to be. On the one hand, birth control allows married couples to relax a little and have sex without fear—something that throughout history many people never got to do. (Just pick up a diary from nineteenth-century America if you want to get inside the head of women who love their husbands, love their children, and love sex, but are terrified of getting pregnant again; not simply because they don't want to spend their entire adult life pregnant or nursing, but also because childbirth was dangerous for nineteenth-century women, as it continues to be today for women without adequate medical care all around the world.)

But if contraception invites us to be carefree, it also encourages us to be people who think we can control and schedule everything, including the creation of our families, down to the month, down to the week. And, most important, it invites us to be people who have utterly separated sex from procreation.

Intuition and observation of people's everyday experiences having sex reminds us how sex, conception, and marriage are connected to one another. Most of us who have had premarital sex will tell you that we usually hoped not to get pregnant. Married people, too, may often have sex hoping not to get pregnant, but *in general* an unplanned pregnancy in a marriage is not quite the same fluster-busting, terror-inducing conundrum that unplanned pregnancies often are for single women. In this observation lies a critique of the ad in *Vogue*. When the ads promise that you can separate sex from procreation, they are telling something close to the truth, technologically. The problem is, they aren't telling the truth theologically.

Christian tradition has historically articulated a threefold purpose for sex: sex is meant to be unitive, procreative, and sacramental. That means, in simpler language, that sex is meant to unite two people, it is meant to lead to children, and it is meant to recall, and even reenact, the promise that God makes to us and that we make to one another in the marriage vow—that is, we promise one another fidelity, and God's Spirit promises a presence that will uphold us in our radical and crazy pledge of lifelong faithfulness.

Each of these three ends of sex has a basis in scripture. The unitive aspect is hinted at in Genesis 2:23, when Adam says that Eve is "bone of my bones and flesh of my flesh." The procreative purpose is also spelled out in Genesis, in God's instruction to be fruitful and multiply. Finally, the sacramental end of sex is implied in Ephesians 5:32, when Paul, having offered a set of guidelines for how husbands and wives should relate to one another, says, "This is a profound mystery—but I am talking about Christ and the church." At first blush, it seems like something of a non sequitur. But, in fact, it tells us what marriage, and marital sex, is: a small patch of experience that gives us our best glimpse of the radical fidelity and intimacy of God and the church.

These three purposes—the unitive, sacramental, and procreative—are deeply interwoven with one another. Openness to children reshapes how we experience and understand sex; procreative possibility changes the way sex is unitive and sacramental. The unitivity of sex, for example, looks different when we remember that unitive sex might produce kids. Without the possibility of procreation, sex can quickly become part of a romantic two-ness, wherein the couple simply becomes more and more deeply interested in one another. The prospect of procreation reconfigures unity, forcing the couple out of themselves, out of a potentially suffocating and selfish oneness, and toward another—toward a stranger, a neighbor, a baby whom they might welcome into their home. When procreation is possible, unitive sex is fruitful beyond simply the couple themselves. (This procreative potential is one thing that keeps marriage from becoming, in Kierkegaard's candid phrase, an ingrown toenail.)

So, too, the possibility of procreation affects how we understand the sacramental aspect of married love and sex, for, again, procreation redirects the lover's attention beyond the spouse, beyond the marriage bed. This is the way sacraments are always meant to work: the Eucharist happens at the table of the body of believers, but we do not stay put at the table; we take Communion with one another so that we might be equipped to follow Christ's injunction to go out into the world. The same is true with baptism—we are washed clean not so that we can preen over our purity and cleanliness, but so that we can go into the world with the unwashed. And sex that is open to procreation is sex that pushes us to be other-directed, that pushes us to leave the bed and journey into the household, and the wider community.

Of course, it is possible for sex without procreation to be incarnate, sacramental, and other-directed. Consider a husband who is sterile, or a wife who is past menopause—these marriages can be as open and hospitable as a marriage that produces children (although that openness and hospitality may require a different level of intention). Nonetheless, experience, nature, and scripture suggest that there is a deep connection between the work of sex and the possibility of procreation.

Technologically effective birth control has severed those connections. We can reaffirm them without necessarily landing at the Roman Catholic position—we can, for example, say that the whole of a married couple's sex life needs to be open to procreation, but each and every sex act need not be. And we can worry about technology's separation of sex and procreation because we see that it does violence to what sex is finally about.

Lie #2: You Shouldn't Marry for Sex

My student Camille dropped into my office a few weeks ago. She's twenty-two, she's a killer tennis player, and she makes a mean batch of chocolate chip cookies to boot.

Camille has been dating a guy named Dean for about a year and a half, and they've been doing a heroic job of falling in love, being normal twenty-somethings, and staying chaste. They've also been talking about marriage.

Camille's parents, it should be noted, are divorced. Camille was raised in the church, but her mom more or less dropped out of the Christian scene after Camille's dad left. Camille and her mom have had their ups and downs, but on the whole they are close. Camille calls home once or twice a week for a recipe, or to ask for advice. And usually the advice is sound. But, with all due respect to Camille's mom, I disagreed with the advice Mom gave this week.

"Mom knows Dean and I are thinking about getting married," Camille told me, "and she said I should wait. She said I should know myself and him better before leaping into anything, and that if the issue was sex, we should just go ahead and have sex, rather than rushing into marriage."

That maternal advice is wildly different from what most moms would have said a generation or two ago. What my own mother was told by her mother was the exact opposite—if you have sex before marriage, no one will want to marry you.

From my perspective, neither of these moms got it quite right. They were both reaching for an ethic of sex and marriage that would serve their daughters well, but they both offered advice that is ultimately inadequate to the task. My grandmother, God rest her soul, was wise in wanting to help my mother guard her chastity, but we miss out when we (especially we women) think of chastity as a cudgel—*I'm staying chaste so that I can successfully trap a man.*

Camille's mom, though understandably eager to make sure that Camille makes a happy and stable match, is also missing the mark. Her advice, I think, not only mistakes the reality of sex, it also reflects a distorted picture of what marriage is and who sustains it.

Camille's mom is not alone. She's simply reiterating a set of assumptions about sex and marriage that have become widespread. A columnist in the *Washington Post* recently gave voice to the common wisdom. He began by noting that Americans now marry later and later—in the mid-1960s, the average

American man was married at 22, the average woman at 20. The median age at which women marry is now 25.1, and for men, 27. The columnist then looked askance at those who, in the face of these statistics, would really ask people to put off sex until marriage. "I wonder if those who seriously advocate abstinence until marriage would prefer to see the marriage age come down. . . . Our youth are less inclined than they were some decades ago to marry hastily, perhaps to the wrong person. Instead, most young Americans wish to be sure that they have found the appropriate mate so that they may create an honorable and viable union. It is difficult to argue with such motivation."

The reasons we give for delaying marriage are entirely understandable. We want to make sure we know ourselves. We want to put away a little money before tying the knot. We want to see the world, or finish college, or graduate from law school before making a time-consuming domestic commitment to another person. Children whose parents have divorced, especially, may want to make sure that they know themselves and their potential mates, to make sure that they won't replicate their parents' mistake.

But these impulses, while perhaps laudable, speak to a distorted understanding of marriage. The anxious parent who wants her college-aged daughter to postpone marriage rightly recognizes that people change a lot in their early twenties. But what that parent perhaps fails to recognize is that there is no point at which we can be sure. There is no age at which we truly know ourselves, and there is no length of courtship after which we really know our sweetie. To underscore that making a marriage is not about making an informed, rational calculation is not to suggest that in an ideal world, high school seniors would marry arbitrarily and hope for the best. It is not to join the chorus on Christian college campuses that sings about having a "ring by spring." Rather, it is to remember that marriage is not merely an exercise in finding the perfect mate; though the companionate marriage has reigned triumphant for these last two centuries, marriage is not only about companionship. It is about children, and household economy, and stability. And marriage is also about God. No matter how clearly we see ourselves and our fiancés, marriage will prove difficult. We will both change. We will argue, and feel broken, and wonder why we ever married in the first place—and it is God who will sustain us in those spells.

Marriage is also about sex; it is about desire. If the *Washington Post* columnist articulates a distorted understanding of marriage, he even more forcefully puts forward a distorted understanding of desire. The church is often just as guilty of misconstruing desire. Consider the confused message we Christians sometimes articulate: we live in a sex-saturated world, there's nothing we can do about it; you shouldn't have sex till you're married; you shouldn't marry till you're absolutely sure—sure of yourself, sure you know your mate well. The unspoken implication is either that single Christians are somehow immune from sexual desire, or that sexual desire just isn't that important.

I think the opposite is true: desire is profoundly important. Important enough to reorder your life around. And that is why I advised Camille and Dean to get married, and promised to toast them when they did.

Lie #3: How You Dress Doesn't Matter

One of my dearest, oldest friends has recently converted to Islam. Her conversion was not sudden, but it still shocks me whenever I think about it. Caroline is from Vermont, and she looks like a J. Crew model, striking, very WASPy. I try to imagine her clipped New England vowels translated into the glottal stops of Arabic. I look at the pictures she sends from Dubai, and wait for my eyes to refocus and adjust to the picture of leggy Caroline cloaked in a hijab, her face peering out from the folds of cloth like a moon, like a nun's face encased in a wimple. You cannot see the lines of her body in these pictures, or her strawberry hair; just her face.

It is a marked contrast to what I see when I look out my window. I see stomachs and thighs and shoulders and ankles and wrists, legs and midriffs and elbows. I see that we dress very differently, that we barely dress at all. Griff teaches tenth-grade English at a Christian school. There's a dress code, but it is enforced only sporadically. He says his girls—and they are still girls, they are only fifteen—wear low-slung hip-huggers and it is hard for passersby not to notice that they are also wearing thongs. On a trip to L.A., I meet a woman who teaches eighth grade in a public school. She says that her students, too, wear the hip-hugging, low-riding pants, "but," she says, "they don't know how to wear them properly. The pants always sneak down too far." I sip my glass of water and suggest it is not that the girls don't know how to wear them properly, but that they are too young to wear hip-huggers properly. "They're thirteen. They don't yet have hips to hug."

I'm not a member of the modesty brigade. I enjoy strolling across a college campus and seeing women sunning in shorts and bathing suits—to me, it bespeaks festivity and youth. I myself run around town in tank tops and don't think twice. I'm not wild about my legs, but sometimes, just for fun, I wear a shorter skirt than usual (my usual is ankle-length, so shorter means knee-length).

But modesty, it seems to me, bears addressing, and not merely because it has become something of a hot topic in recent years. Rather, it bears discussing because we seem, as a society, to be losing the ability to discern why clothes matter, and what clothing is appropriate when.

I began to wonder about our sartorial sensibility when my friend Anne was in the hospital. Anne's five-year-old daughter Henrietta needed some new spring clothes, and, since Anne was recuperating from surgery, I volunteered to take Henrietta shopping. Henrietta and I went from shop to shop, but I couldn't see anything for her that I thought was appropriate. The kindergarten set, it appears, is wearing the same low-riding, midriff-revealing tops and trousers that their big sisters and moms are sporting. At least, the working-class and middling kindergartners are. All the affordable shops, in other words, specialize in revealing outfits and tight skirts. Wealthy daughters, whose parents can afford to shop at Hanna Andersson and Nordstrom, still get little girl clothes—crinolines and dresses and smocking. But we apparently expect their less-well-off cousins to start dressing for sex early. If you're rich, you get to be shielded from the objectifications and ravages of the culture; you get the safeties of both childhood and purity. Poor girls get no such protections.

Christians have long worried about clothing. In the 1920s, some preachers thought the beaded necklaces and fringed dresses of bobbed-hair flappers guaranteed licentiousness. Today those dresses look tame. But if fashions have changed, the questions we bring to bear on modesty have not.

The Christian imperative toward modest dressing usually falls squarely on the shoulders of women. Women are told to cover up because if you run around town shaking your hips and flashing your midriff, your very body will become a stumbling block in the path of some poor man, who will see you and get all hot and bothered and inevitably be led to fantasize, lust, and masturbate.

There's wisdom in that code, of course. Seeing attractive women about town may turn some men on, and the Christian idiom of communal responsibility suggests that women can't shake their heads and say, "Well, that's the guy's problem." Rather, we are to take care of and look out for one another, and for women that might mean thinking about how your male colleagues or friends react when you show off your shapely thighs. (For that matter, men could do with a little covering up. The hordes of college-aged men who jog shirtless through my neighborhood every evening are a stumbling block for plenty of women.)

But there are also some problems with the old notion that if women would just cover up, men could be pure; and if Christians needn't abandon modesty, we could rethink the way we talk about it. We can easily slip from encouraging women to help support their male comrades in their pursuit of chastity and fidelity, to insisting that women are singularly responsible for male sexual behavior. This insistence finds its most pernicious expression in the suggestion that female victims of sexual violence are somehow responsible for the crimes committed against them, that if they hadn't been wearing that short, seductive skirt, they wouldn't have gotten raped. Nor does this discourse do men any favors. It lets them off the hook, suggesting that men are just beasts, animals who can't be expected to control their bodies. Men aren't responsible, so women have to be responsible for them.

Those who would criticize a culture of immodesty need to castigate not individual women but the marketplace that produces the clothes women wear. Women are forced to think about modesty not because they are women—not because they are temptresses, Eves determined to bring down good guys—but because the market has sexualized women's clothing. Recently, Griff and I had a houseguest, a twenty-nine-year-old lawyer who crashed on our sofa en route to a courtroom in South Carolina. She wandered around in the morning, hunting for coffee, wearing a neckline-plunging, fitted, and flattering red T-shirt. Griff later said he'd wished she would cover up. He said he had trouble interacting with her as a person and not just a pair of breasts. Fair enough. But was this solely our houseguest's fault? She'd probably just grabbed the red top off the rack at Old Navy. It looked good. It was affordable. She bought what was available, and what was available was sexy. Try finding a truly modest summer frock that doesn't make you look like a sack of potatoes—it isn't impossible, but it also isn't the easiest thing in the world either. (This is one reason I haunt vintage clothing shops. Women's clothing in the 1930s and 1950s was so much better—flattering, feminine lines, shapely and chic, but modest to a fault.) Women, of course, can make individual choices about what to purchase, but the greater structural and social fault lies with a fashion industry that—perhaps because women are so often seen as the consumers in our society, or perhaps because the world's leading fashion mavens are men, or perhaps because fashion simply does its part in sustaining a centuries-long objectification of women's bodies—specializes in sexualizing women's dress.

The shapers of haute couture in Paris and New York have begun to sex up men's clothes, too. In the 1990s, men's suits moved from the big lapel, double-breasted, boxy affairs of the 1980s to tighter, British lines that highlighted an idealized masculine physique. By the millennium, this look had trickled down from the sleek suits that fashion guru Tom Ford created for Gucci to the tight tops and body-hugging trousers of Banana Republic's menswear. (Ford summarized the trend in a 2001 interview, declaring that "Menswear is moving much faster than it has ever before. Men are finally accepting the role of sexual attraction and are more comfortable with it.") At the University of Virginia, I often spy male undergrads heading to the library wearing sleeveless T-shirts, inevitably recalling (if also falling short of) the raw sexuality of Marlon Brando in *A Streetcar Named Desire*. So men too would do well to resist the imperatives of an industry happy to sell the erotic to anyone with plastic or cash.

Modest dress—appropriate dress, if you will—is not simply about covering up potentially enticing body parts. What's lost when we let it all hang out is not simply the allure—or the Victorian primness—of modesty. What's lost is a whole vocabulary, a sartorial liturgy. What's lost is the recognition that how we dress shapes how we carry ourselves, how we interact with others, how we engage our communities and institutions. (For a stark illustration of how clothing marks and molds us, see the movie *Thirteen*, an autobiographical film about a Los Angeles teen who goes from good girl to heroin-shooting sexpot. Her first step in that direction is to change clothes—she swaps her little girl clothes for miniskirts and tube tops.)

Casual Fridays, I think, capture some of our society's confusion about clothes. Professional workplaces have dress codes in part because managers know that how we dress shapes our behavior. If we dress up, if we dress professionally, we are more likely to behave professionally, to treat others with respect and be treated likewise. A few years ago, when employers all over corporate America said employees could dress down on the last day of the work week, workers were thrilled. No more constricting ties on Fridays, no more annoying pantyhose; trade in those suits for capris and blue jeans.

I have to admit that I find this trend puzzling (which is not to say that when I worked in a newsroom I didn't appreciate the lax Friday dress codes). Maybe I'm a glutton for consistency, but it seems to me that if it is important for people to dress up four days of the week—because formal clothing truly shapes how we comport ourselves, how we understand our work and our duty—then it is important for us to dress up on Fridays too. Conversely, if employers find that people are happier, work better, and are more present when dressed in blue jeans, then we should scotch the silly dress codes the other four days. Either clothing really does some constructive work, or it doesn't. Either we're fooling ourselves on Fridays, or we're fooling ourselves the other four days. Perhaps we see in casual Fridays that we've lost our insight into the way clothing shapes us; perhaps, without the sense that clothes make the man (and woman), clothing becomes merely an exercise in conspicuous consumption.

We see the two trends—low-cut blouse meets casual dress at work—twinned in many contemporary offices. A Sears, Roebuck design manager recently observed that today's work attire tends toward a "sexy . . . almost trashy interpretation of fashion." And fashion historians say the current clothes are different even from the tight and revealing fashions of the 1970s, the last decade when sexy was in. "Then that kind of outfit was for partying," explains the University of Kentucky's Susan Bordo. "Now it has a place in the office." The assumption on the part of those who dress like sex kittens at work is apparently that clothes don't mean much. A head honcho at Barneys New York explained to a *New York Times* fashion reporter that "fashion has lost its meaning as a signifier. . . . Someone [who is] showing lots of leg" is not necessarily trying to send a message about sex. Ask women themselves, and they'll say their office clothing *does* have a message—not "I want to sleep with you," but "I've made it to the big leagues; don't you dare breathe a word about how I'm dressed." As one twenty-seven-year-old marketing exec, who regularly wore capri pants and mules to work, explained, "I have an MBA under my belt. I work hard. I don't have to prove anything." Another young working woman, defending her clingy polyester tops and knee-high boots, said, "I know it might not be 100 percent appropriate, but I fault those who would judge me on what I wear." With fashion, as with the rest of life, what these employees *intend* may be irrelevant. For their clothing tells stories—about both sex and work—and their outfits shape them whether they intend it or not.

I've especially noticed the relationship between clothing and behavior in the classroom. I get ticked when students come to class dressed in their gym clothes. I get ticked because this bespeaks their priorities—the real event is the workout on the Stairmaster, which will happen after class. And I get ticked because their casual clothing permits a casual attitude, a slouching, an irreverence. But it is not my students' fault. Some of their teachers wear blue jeans to class, so why should the students dress up? They are, as it were, just following suit.

The church has been complicit in teaching that there is no propriety to dress. We used to dress to the nines on Sunday morning. In the 1960s, that began to change—students and surfers and Jesus freaks began turning up at church in jeans and sandals. That's all well and good—I'm not suggesting the church copy five-star restaurants and post a maître d' at the door to hand out jackets and ties to men who show up in T-shirts. Everyone, even those who disdain or can't afford spiffy suits, should be welcome in church. But perhaps we've erred on the side of casual. I've noticed that I worship differently when I'm wearing more formal, fancy clothes. I'm more inclined toward reverence. I'm readier to meet a king. The prayers I pray when I'm wearing my pj's are, not surprisingly, often more intimate, and there is a place for pj prayers—but that place may not always be church. We Christians in our institutional churches so want people to come worship with us on Sunday morning that we hesitate to impose a dress code upon them. And yet what appears welcoming, what seems hospitable, may in fact be a failure. It's God, after all, that the people are coming for, and helping them dress appropriately may be part of preparing them to meet Him.

There is, it seems to me, a certain power in modest dressing, an assertion that though my body is beautiful, I am more than a sex object designed for your passing entertainment. But the power of dressing is also the power of narrative. For our clothes tell stories, and it would be naïve and irresponsible to pretend otherwise. Clothes tell stories about sex and chastity, to be sure, but they also narrate a stance toward our environments; our dress suggests a set of priorities. That is why we enjoy clothing so much, of course—because we reinvent ourselves and our narratives when we try out a new look. So the question for Christians is not an absolute one about skirt length, but rather something about communication. What stories do we want to tell ourselves and others through our choices of clothing?

Lie #4: Good Sex Can't Happen in the Humdrum Routine of Marriage

Our popular culture sends us some pretty mixed messages about the importance of sex. On the one hand, we're told that sex is the most important thing there is. We find an interpretation of sexuality even in the seemingly innocuous and terribly commonplace phrase *sex life*. Hard work and perseverance, cautions one therapist, are required if you want "a totally revamped sex life. . . . Whatever you do, don't wait for a bad sex life to get better all by itself." Mavis Cheek's novel promises to divulge all about *The Sex Life of My Aunt*. Another popular novel even ascribes such a life to bees: "They do not have a riotous sex life themselves. A hive suggests cloister more than

bordello." The phrase is revealing. A sex life is something we
have, something we can make and remake, something we can
mold. And a sex life is also basic, fundamental; when we attach
another noun to the word *life*—love life, prayer life—we de-
note something of the utmost importance, something essential,
something basic to life itself.

At the same time, the shapers of popular culture tell us that
sex is meaningless. In an episode of the hit sitcom *Friends*,
Monica asks her new paramour, "So, we can still be friends,
and have sex?" "Sure," he replies, "it'll just be something we
do together, like racquetball." It could be a tagline for our age:
Sex: It's just like racquetball. It's no big deal. It's just a game.

In Monica's world, sex need not be understood as anything
more than thrills and fun. There is no shortage of movies—
wildly successful blockbusters like *American Pie* and highbrow
artsy flicks like *Y Tu Mama Tambien*—that depict sexual intercourse as intense pleasure quests. Anyone who has turned
on daytime television knows this only too well. Shows like
Jerry Springer are essentially daily parades of people who have
figured out yet another way to transform sex into a spectacle
and instance of lurid fascination. A sophisticated cultural critic
might say that American consumer culture, with its emphasis on
enjoyment and novel experiences, has turned sex into nothing
more than another form of entertainment. It is not too much
to say that as recreational pursuits have become more extreme
(how many iterations of power yoga and extreme sports can
one nation take?), sex has followed suit.

Of course, what I have just been doing—pointing out the
manifold ways sex takes the form of a frenetic hedonism—is
awfully easy work. It is also far from original: there is probably no more frequent target for social and religious critics
than American culture's loose sexual mores. And though critics who espouse this piece of conventional wisdom get some
things right, they do not say all there is to be said about the
place of sex in larger American culture.

For amid the contradictory messages about the importance
of sex—it is vitally important, but it is just a game—is another

message about sex, a definition of what great sex is. Great sex is readily available. It is unyoked from outdated and restrictive moralities. Above all, it is romantic and otherworldly. It happens in an alternate universe, a world removed from the ins-and-outs of daily domestic life. Great sex, which once was assumed to occur by definition only in marriage, is now understood as something that's threatened by marriage. Magazines and advice columnists tell us that the best sex happens away from our ordinary lives. The best sex happens between carefree young men and women as a prelude, or coda, to a swanky night on the town. Great sex can happen when we're dating, when we're trolling bars and parties (or the halls of the Russell Senate Building) looking for a one-night stand. But great sex is much harder to come by in the comfortable bedrooms of ordinary married Americans.

After all, nothing stands between Jessica Cutler and fantastic frolics with six sexual partners. But the list of things that prevent an ordinary husband and wife (not to mention an ordinary mom and dad) from having great sex is endless. The predictability gets in the way. The routine. The dishes in the dishwasher. The pitter-patter of little feet. The argument you had yesterday about where to spend Thanksgiving. Your resentment that she bought yet another pair of black shoes with your hard-earned money. All these trials and tribulations of daily life get in the way of Mr. and Mrs. getting it on.

According to the magazines, our married couple needs to send the kids to their grandparents' and head to a B&B. Or they could, as one bride's guide to marriage suggests, "Buy some 'dirty dice.' Roll them on the sheets of your bed and then do what they say to do." (The same guide urges women to "Wear the thong even though it's lace and really scratches.") At the very least, married couples should vary the time of day they have sex, or the location—perhaps some seduction on the stovetop (make sure it's off first) would spice things up.

This notion of sex as a flight from ordinary time and the quotidian interactions between husband and wife pervades popular culture. When *Redbook* offers women "16 Ways to

Free Your Mind for Great Sex" or "51 Secrets to a Sexier Marriage"—magazines' sex gurus urge wives to wear a soft color that "projects vulnerability," and to consider microwaving a towel and then wrapping up in it; hopefully, the towel's warmth will release some of your stress—it is assumed that great sex is not only unmoored from ordinary domestic life, but is actually at odds with domestic life. For great sex you need to take a bubble bath, slip into something silky, and sip a little champagne. Great sex can't happen if you're thinking about the lunches you have to pack in the morning or if you can hear your child get up to go to the bathroom. The realities of hearth and home threaten to tame sexual desire, so our popular culture has turned sex into a bulwark against and a refuge from the commonplace and ordinary practices of marriage. It has created a falsely romantic ideal of sexual love, and has radically removed sex and love from the day-to-day routines and domesticities of the household.

The landscape of contemporary sexual ethics resembles a battlefield of competing sexual mores. Both modes of sexual practice—sex as only a meaningless but dazzling physical experience, and sex as a flight from hearth and home—are widely held in American life. Too often we assume that contemporary American sexual life is a one-dimensional world of licentious prurience. Yet it may be more important for contemporary Christian ethics to constructively engage secular romanticism than to righteously denounce sexual libertinism. It is, after all, pretty easy for us Christians to distinguish ourselves from the sex-is-recreation ethic. The real question is not whether we can counter the message that sex is just like racquetball, but whether we can also articulate a Christian alternative to the regnant ideal of sex as an otherworldly, illicit romance, an escape from quotidian, domestic life. The Christian, in other words, can not only diagnose profligacy as immoral, but also diagnose modern romanticism as fundamentally unsustainable, as something that militates against Christian love properly and constructively conceived. This romanticism, and particularly the way it construes sex, does not allow for nurturing the sorts of values that marriage and sexual intercourse, when understood as distinctly Christian practices, must be made to honor.

As theologian David McCarthy argues in his provocative book *Sex and Love in the Home*, a Christian ethics of sex, love, and marriage needs to reconceive sex and love as practices that exist ideally *only* within the basic prosaic rhythms of house and home: candlelight, long-stemmed roses, and lingerie can't sustain love, but domestic economies can. This is not, at root, an argument based on realism or expediency. Rather, the point is that it is only through household practices that Christians come to embody the Christian virtues of mutual care, forgiveness, generosity, community, interdependence, and reconciliation. Our humanity cannot be separated from the moments of joy, anger, friendship, sadness, attention, confusion, tedium, and wonder that unfold over time and in specific places. Human intimacy is hammered out on an anvil made of nothing more, in McCarthy's phrase, than the "day-to-day ebb and flow of common endeavors, joys, and struggles of love in the home." Love, sex, and marriage, to be theological, must drink from the very same wells. Love, sex, and marriage, to partake in their transcendent mission of revealing God's grace, must embrace life's decidedly untranscendent daily goings-on.

In a Christian landscape, what's important about sex is nurtured when we allow sex to be ordinary. This does not mean that sex will not be meaningful. Its meaning, instead, will partake in the variety of meanings that ordinary life offers. Sex needs to be clumsy. It should at times feel awkward. It should be an act we engage in for comfort. It should also be allowed to hold any number of anxieties—the sorts of anxieties, for instance, we might feel about our child's progress in school, or our ability to provide sustenance for our family. Sex becomes another way for two people to realistically engage the strengths and foibles of each other. Not only sexual intercourse is transformed as we allow it to take on the varieties of the commonplace; the varieties of the commonplace themselves are transformed as well. If we allow sex to be ordinary, we might better understand that human love is forged in, say, time spent cooking together, or in picking up our loved one's laundry, or in calming our children's fears. Through sexual practice, we come to find each other fallible, and we come to love each other for the way we see each other creating very human lives out of those very fallibilities.

A household conceived in Christ's image is, as I suggested in chapter three, far from limited to the interactions between husband and wife. The Christian household is a distinctly communal venture, connected to neighbors and strangers and loved ones. In McCarthy's phrase, Christian sexual intercourse is a "set of bodily activities where we come to belong and to be set, irreplaceably, within an expanding context of family, friends, and neighbors. Conjugal unions . . . do not set us apart (through romantic moments), but uniquely in the middle of things."

What, more practically, does this really mean? What might it mean to open up married sexual life to the varieties of winds that shape our lives together? What might it look like to open up sexuality to our neighbors?

The sorts of challenges that attend creating community, all of which revolve around the complexities of being responsible to the other, are present in our sexual lives. The stuff of creating community—which we experience as work, as at times more than we can bear, as taking an extraordinary amount of time, and as requiring us to make ourselves present to the other—is the stuff of creating a Christian sexuality. To say that marriage ought not to be a private endeavor is to say more than that Christian marriage is transformed into a communal venture when we expose the deep inner workings of our marriages to members of our communities. We also need to expose the deep inner workings of our communities to our marriages; we need to take what we know about being a community and bring it to bear on sex.

A critique of romantic passion need not be a battle against all conceptions of passion. Just as sexuality survives, and survives well, within the household, so does passion. Passion and desire situated within the household are transformed into emotional manifestations of the strength, resiliency, and commitment that mark the best moments of human cooperation.

Our task is not to cultivate moments when *eros* can whisk us away from our ordinary routines, but rather to love each other as *eros* becomes imbedded in, and transformed by, the daily warp and woof of married life. For in household sexuality, we see the ways our daily human struggles offer the only language we have to call ourselves to God's grace.

5

STRAIGHT TALK II

Lies the Church Tells about Sex

Christians should keep talking about sex so that they can learn to speak about it more adequately, that is, more theologically.

—Mark Jordan

Cosmo and *Maxim* aren't the only places that lie. The Christian community—the church—also perpetuates some false ideas about sex. The church's intention, no doubt, is noble and laudable, but in its fervent determination to preserve sex for marriage in a broader culture that is ever more hostile to Christian sexual ethics, the church tells a few fibs of its own.

Lie #1: Premarital Sex Is Guaranteed to Make You Feel Lousy

A theme that runs through many Christian conversations about sex is the insistence that if we have premarital sex, we'll feel bad about it. If we go to bed with our boyfriend, we will feel wracked with guilt, or, even more likely, we'll wake up in the morning feeling lonely and bereft.

To be sure, that is sometimes true. Sometimes after a one-night stand, or after sex with your girlfriend of two years, or even after kissing a guy you don't know very well, you feel lousy. You feel ashamed, or alienated, or lonely, or just plain down in the dumps.

But sometimes it is not true. Sometimes, even after sinful sex, a person will feel fantastic. Consider one unmarried woman's reflections on her first sexual experience: "Because I felt so safe and comfortable, it was a beautiful experience, which grew into more fun and playfulness and touching and love throughout our four-year relationship. . . . [When I told my dad I'd had sex, he] wanted me to feel guilty, but I didn't; I felt sure of myself and happy in my relationship." Or this: "I had never felt this vulnerable, open, and receptive. . . . I felt grateful and in love." Or: "Afterward, I felt blissfully happy and comfortable; it had been like the romantic scene in the movies that never happens in reality, a softly lit, slow-motion, tender entwinement of love."

Even when folks don't feel transformed and enraptured after premarital sex, they don't necessarily feel devastated. A teenager writing to the love-and-sex advice columnist at the Christian magazine *Campus Life* described her initial indifference to premarital sex: "Both my parents were raised Christian, and we went to church Christmas and Easter, but I don't even know a lot of what my religion is about. I know there is an idea that you shouldn't have sex before marriage, but since I hadn't really been following any teachings, I lost my virginity and didn't think anything of it. I think the first time I began to think sex outside of marriage might be wrong was when I slept with my ex-boyfriend's friend. I did this to show my ex-boyfriend that what we had wasn't special. And then it hit me. Sex is supposed to be a special bond between two people." Eventually this young woman came to think that something was wrong with casual sex—but she didn't feel especially bad after she first had sex. In fact she "didn't think anything of it."

It is curious that contemporary Christians often insist that we will necessarily *feel bad* after premarital sex. Jesus understood that we pitiful human beings are often very out of touch with our sins. He makes the point in the parable of the prodigal son. The turning point of that story comes in Luke 15:17 (NRSV): the prodigal, Jesus tells us, "came to himself." Before this moment of turning, of awakening, the prodigal was not in himself at all. And we are often not in ourselves, not aware of our fallen state or the sins we cycle through. St. Augustine riffs on Jesus's wisdom when he reminds his readers that we barely even know that we're fallen, let alone that we constantly sin. Dante sounds the same theme in his *Inferno*. None of the people in Dante's hell, including the great traitor Judas Iscariot, think they have done anything wrong.

The ubiquitous expression "casual sex" suggests how removed we often are from the real work of sex. Even the most sexually conservative folk think nothing of using the phrase "casual sex." But casual sex is a contradiction in terms. Sex—even sex that does not feel intense or meaningful, even sex with someone you don't love—is never truly casual. Christian ethicist Lewis Smedes addresses this question head-on in his book *Sex for Christians*. To understand that sex can never be casual, says Smedes, one must understand what sex really is. Considering 1 Corinthians 6:15–17—the passage in which Paul tells the Corinthians to avoid prostitution—Smedes reminds readers that "behind Paul's vigorous attack on fornication is a positive view of sexual intercourse," and that positive view is that sex "involves two people in a life-union; it is a life-uniting act." This is what sex *is*, not necessarily what sex *seems to be*. It may *seem* casual, but in fact it *is*, always, profound. As Smedes explains, "It does not matter what the two people have in mind. . . . [Sex] unites them in that strange, impossible to pinpoint sense of 'one flesh.' There is no such thing as casual sex, no matter how casual people are about it."

Surprisingly, one of the most powerful articulations I've heard of this came in a Tom Cruise movie, *Vanilla Sky*. Cruise plays a

man-about-town who has finally ended a fling with a beautiful
blonde he was never serious about. But the blonde can't handle
the break-up; her pursuit of Cruise borders on stalking. When
she finally corners him, she utters real wisdom about sex; she is
putting St. Paul in contemporary lingo: "Don't you know that
when you sleep with someone, your body makes a promise
whether you do or not?"

The recognition that sex is "life-uniting" carries with it a
recognition of something even more basic—that human beings
are not fully persons insofar as we are individuals. Rather, we
become true persons in community, in the Body of God. Sex
returns us to that oneness promised in the Book of Genesis—the
communal oneness of "male and female created He them."

Indeed, it is precisely because something really real happens
during sex that sex is so controversial. Even during misordered,
misplaced sex—the tipsy cavorting of hormone-drunk teenagers, say—something real happens. This misordered sex comes
disturbingly close to the moral and spiritual goods that sex
within marriage promises; the teenagers' moonstruck gropings
make us so nervous precisely because they are a perfect parody
of sex as God meant it to be.

So even though "casual sex" is a contradiction in terms, it is
certainly possible to have sex that seems casual, or feels casual.
My friend Julie, who lives in Washington, D.C., tells about a
trip she once took to Boston. While there, she had dinner with
an old college buddy. It was snowing out, and they were tucked
into his apartment with a pot of bouillabaisse and a Louis Arm-
strong CD. After the bouillabaisse and the music, they had sex.
The next morning, Julie's friend made pancakes, they thumbed
through the *Boston Globe*, and Julie went on her way.

Was that sex, in reality, casual? No. Something really happened between Julie and her college mate; their bodies united
themselves in a mysterious and profound, if imperceptible, way.
Imperceptible is the key. The sex may not have been casual, but
Julie will tell you that it certainly *felt* casual. It felt, really, like
nothing. It was fun. She and the Boston man are still friends.
They go out to eat whenever he's in D.C.

Certainly, sometimes premarital sex does *not* feel casual. Sometimes it feels intense. Sometimes, you feel like you are being bonded to a person, and it feels devastating to go home in the morning, or to break up in six months. But occasionally, as with Julie and her jazz-loving colleague, having sex feels no more significant than meeting for a cup of coffee.

Julie's feelings, of course, were deceiving her—which is precisely the point. This is how sin works: it whispers to us about the goodness of something not good. It makes distortions feel good. It tells us we'd be better off with pleasure in hell than sanctification in heaven.

In insisting that premarital sex will make you feel bad, the church is misstating the nature of sin and the nature of our fallen hearts. The plain, sad fact is that we do not always feel bad after we do something wrong. To acknowledge that premarital sex—or any other sinful act—might *feel* good is not to say that premarital sex *is* good. It is rather to say that our feelings are not always trustworthy. Our emotions and our hearts were distorted in the fall, which is one reason we need the community of the church and an articulated Christian ethics in the first place. If our feelings could be trusted—if we felt good every time we did something good, and felt bad every time we did something bad—we would need neither biblical guidelines of right behavior nor a community to help hold us accountable to those biblical standards. In other words, if we felt lousy every time we sinned, there would be a lot less sinning in the world. And if we felt great every time we did something good and worthy and true, there would be a lot more prayer and giving of charity.

To insist that people will *feel terrible* after premarital sex is not only to miss something essential about the way sin's deceptions work, it is also to make a pastoral faux pas. Let's imagine Lillian, a young woman who has heard since puberty that premarital sex will leave her feeling guilt-ridden and lonely. For years, she avoids temptation, but she's come to her mid-twenties, she's not married, she's been dating the same guy for eight months, and eventually, she has sex. Perhaps she will feel horrible, but perhaps she won't. And then Lillian may think "Hmmmm. My pastor has been telling me for a decade that this would feel bad, but it doesn't. Maybe everything else he told me about sex is wrong too." If guilt is the only resource the church has given Lillian to diagnose sin and remain chaste, in the absence of guilt, she will simply keep having sex, not to mention she'll begin to doubt the authority of her pastor.

What the church means to say, I think, is that premarital sex *is* bad for us, even if it happens to *feel* great. In other words, sexual sin is not subjectively felt. Indeed, no realm of sin is always subjectively felt, but sex—intense and complicated endeavor that it is—would seem to be a place where our feelings are among the least reliable. Sex, after all, stands at the intersection of nature and grace. The experience of sex that I can describe and name and talk about is an experience of the natural. My bodily experience might tell me, for example, that sex feels good, that nerve endings have been stimulated, that I like being held. But sex must be read as an experience of a fallen person—and, when sex is rightly ordered, an experience of nature infused by grace. This is why our record of experience is insufficient. My experience of sex is not bad data, but it is incomplete. We may at times feel bland or blasé about premarital sex, not because the sex itself was morally or spiritually neutral, but because we are, after a fashion, sleepwalkers going through our routines, eyes closed to reality as it really is.

Lie # 2: Women Don't Really Want to Have Sex, Anyway

The second myth that pervades Christian conversations about sex—and I should admit that this particular myth really ticks me off—is the notion that while men are randy brutes, raring to leap into bed at the first opportunity, women don't really like sex, and aren't that interested in having sex (premarital or marital). One Christian marriage guide, for example, describes "a young couple, very committed to the Lord, who are engaged to be married" in two weeks. After going to a movie, the young man kisses his fiancée good night, drops her off at home, and then prays, while heading home himself, that the Lord continue to help him discipline his sexual desire: "Lord, there are . . . two more weeks that I'll have to restrain myself. I know Your grace is sufficient, but if You could just let these two weeks zip by I'd certainly be grateful." The young woman is praying too—giving thanks for the "marvelous, glorious evening" and asking God to help her "savor every wedding shower." She cherishes the experience of having "eaten popcorn out of the same sack at the movies. . . . To her, this was such an intimate, special experience that she slipped one of the kernels into the pocket of her sweater so she could press it in her diary." What accounts for the differences between the man's and woman's prayers? "Our popcorn story only begins to illustrates the difference in the sexual makeup of men and women. . . . The difference is so immense that it's difficult to define." In fact, the difference this popcorn story suggests seems pretty straightforward—men don't have emotions, and women don't have libidos.

This idea even affects Christian thinking about parenting: in the introduction to a chapter called "What Girls Need to Know Before They Start Dating," one popular Christian parenting book reminds readers that "from early childhood, [girls'] fantasies are of Prince Charming and motherhood, not sex." By high school "a boy's sex drive . . . may be the strongest driving force in his mind. While girls may have an increase in libido, their thoughts are about nonsexual socialization, dating, fun, parties, holding hands, and maybe kissing. . . . Every mother . . . should teach her daughter what boys are like." The rest of the chapter details just that, telling us that "boys are high-octane sexual creatures." Moms must tell their daughters "not [to] fall for a boy's lies or lines." Apparently moms don't need to talk to daughters about how to control their own desires—just how to fend off the raging bundles of hormones that take their daughters to the movies.

The idea that women aren't that interested in sex is certainly not new, nor is it uncontested. For much of Western history, women were thought to be less rational, and therefore more likely to abandon themselves to passion, than men. But beginning in the seventeenth century, women (in particular, white women) came to be seen as less passionate, less interested in sex, frankly less carnal, than men. Women's "superior delicacy," to borrow the phrase of one English moralist, disinclined women toward sex. By the nineteenth century, moralists and physicians alike held to this new orthodoxy: it was men, not women, who were lustful and lascivious. Women might dispense conjugal favors, but they didn't crave sex.

Current opinion—popular and social-scientific—suggests that men's and women's libidos are actually quite similar. In their study *The Good Marriage*, Judith Wallerstein and Sandra Blakeslee found that in a quarter of marriages wives wanted more sex than their husbands, in another quarter men wanted more sex, and half "were evenly matched in desire." Over 57 percent of 800 women surveyed in 2004 said "they want more sex, no matter how much they are actually having." One respondent wrote, "Everyone says that men have higher sex drives, but among my friends the reverse is actually true. My girlfriends and I always laugh about how we have to seduce our boyfriends to get as much sex as we want." Adolescent girls are exuberantly, daringly sexual. As Sharon Lamb puts it in *The Secret Life of Girls*, "Teenage girls today engage in sex earlier and speak more freely about their sexual exploits" than ever before. "Girls, like boys, are deeply sexual, deeply aggressive creatures." Indeed, corner the mom of a teenager and she will tell you that in American high schools today, girls seem to be *more* relationally and sexually aggressive than boys; girls are the ones calling, girls are initiating dates, girls are doing the chasing.

It is worth noting that men's and women's sexual desires fluctuate with circumstance and life stage. As I researched this book, a number of male pastors told me that many of the married couples they counsel wrestle with an imbalance of sexual desire: the men want to have sex more often than the women. I don't doubt this. The women in question are often nursing newborns, or running after toddlers all day, or working the "second shift"—holding down a salaried job in the world plus shouldering the bulk of domestic labor at home. These women are exhausted, not to mention tactilely supersaturated with the grabbing touch of kids. But to make assumptions about and formulate pastoral guidance for unmarried women based on the experiences of married moms makes little sense. It's no surprise that Jane Doe, who has three children under the age of eight and a full-time job as a paralegal, isn't overwhelmed with sexual desire night after night; but her exhaustion and lack of desire does not tell us very much about the libido, expectations, and desires of Jane's younger, single sister.

Getting into a debate about who is more interested in sex—men or women, teenage boys or teenage girls—is futile. It is sufficient simply to acknowledge that women have libidos. Many unmarried women want to have sex, not simply because they are trying to please their boyfriends, but because sex is enjoyable for women, too. Women's bodies (like men's bodies) are wired for sexual pleasure. Women (like men) crave the emotional connectivity that sex seems to offer.

We Christians are not doing anyone any good when we perpetuate the notion that women don't really want to have sex. In fact, to insist that women lack sexual desire is really to do a disservice to teenage girls and women. When we follow the advice of the parenting guide I quoted above, we fail to prepare women for some of the real challenges and pressures they will meet as they try to live chastely. Are many women likely to encounter men who pressure them to have sex? Sure. But they are also likely to encounter pressures that may seem even more urgent and be even more persuasive—the pressures of their own bodies and their own desires.

Lie #3: Bodies (and Sex) are Gross, Dirty, or Just Plain Unimportant

In chapter two, we talked a little about Gnosticism—the heretical idea that our bodies are bad, or that our bodies are unimportant, or that our bodies are not part of what really makes us human. This anxiety about bodies runs counter to the radical embodiment of the Christian story—which unequivocally proclaims that we were created with bodies, that God called our bodies good, that Jesus came as a body and saved us with His body, and that He is and we will be resurrected as bodies. As Paul tells the Corinthians: "You were bought with a price. So glorify God in your body."

And yet Christians have been beset by ambivalence about bodily matters, especially sex, from Paul's day to the present. Many of us share a sneaking suspicion that bodies don't matter. Or we're confused about what role bodies play in our spiritual lives. Or we think of Christianity as something we do with our souls and minds and hearts; our bodies get sort of left behind. (To wit, an informal poll conducted by a friend who teaches at a small Christian college. He asked one of his classes how many of the students believed in a bodily resurrection, and of the thirty-five students, only five said they did.)

The screen on which the contemporary church works out its anxieties about bodies is sexuality. Too often, Christians' aching discomfort with bodies gets transmitted into how we do sex; our anxiety about bodies morphs into anxiety about, or repugnance toward, sexual desire and sexual acts. If we fear our bodies because they are undisciplined and contingent, messy and willful, we then get especially freaked out about sex, which is one of the places where our bodies are most willful and messiest. When the body becomes something to escape from, the sexual body becomes something to vilify.

I want to tell you a story about my friends Charlie and Suzanne. They should have had a picture-perfect wedding night. They had both grown up in strong Christian families, and they had both determined as high-schoolers to save sex for marriage. They met their senior year of college, and were engaged eight months later. And they dutifully refrained from having sex before they were married; in fact, before they got engaged they did no more than kiss.

Their honeymoon was to be spent at a quaint cottage in the countryside. Friends and family had suggested they go to Paris or Rome, but Suzanne laughed and said, "We'll go to Paris later when we might want to spend time at museums and bistros." In other words, they'd waited for sex and assumed they'd want to spend most of their honeymoon in bed.

But their wedding night was, in Suzanne's words, "a disaster." Though Charlie was eager to make the beast with two backs (that's Shakespeare's felicitous phrase, not my own), she simply did not want to have sex. "I did have sex, of course, because . . . that's what you do." But she wasn't happy about it. Nor did she want to have sex much during their first three years of marriage, until they started meeting with a counselor employed by their church. "I knew there would be a learning curve with sex," says Suzanne, "but I thought that meant learning about mechanics. What I really had to learn was that sex is OK—that it is OK to desire my husband."

Rather than spending our unmarried years stewarding and disciplining our desires, we have become ashamed of them. We persuade ourselves that the desires themselves are horrible. This can have real consequences if we do get married. We spend years guarding our virginity, but find, upon getting married, that we cannot just flip a switch. Now that sex is licit, sanctioned—even blessed by our community—we are stuck with years of work (and sometimes therapy) to unlearn a gnostic anxiety about sex; to learn, instead, that sex is good.

Charlie and Suzanne's experience is an illustration of the Christian approach to chastity gone wrong. The problem is not that they were chaste before marriage, but rather that somewhere along the way Suzanne learned that sex, even once you are married, is bad. I doubt that Suzanne ever heard a sermon where the pastor said, "Sex is bad! Sex is evil!" In fact, these days most church folk who speak or write about sex bend over backward to insist that *married* sex is great. But somehow the church still manages to convey anxiety and discomfort about sex writ large. In subtle ways we hear that the body is not important. We don't get much teaching on caring for our bodies or thinking about the food we eat, and as teenagers and single adults, we are told over and over not to have sex, but no one ever encourages us to be bodily or sensual in some appropriate way. Thus, many of us find it hard, once we marry, to accord sex respect, dignity, pleasure, or value; we've learned to reduce sex, and everything else bodily, to something that has only utilitarian function. As Christian sex therapist Douglas E. Rosenau explains in *A Celebration of Sex for Newlyweds*, "You have so carefully guarded your sexuality and set such rigid boundaries that you have repressed your sexual feelings. . . . Nudity and sexual activity may be scary or even repulsive at first."

Women more than men, it's worth noting, seem captive to the notion that sex is wrong. As Wheaton College sociologist Lisa Graham McMinn has written, "Some women bring inhibitions into their marriages that emerged from broken images and experiences with their sexuality. When the idea that good girls don't like sex is combined with the commitment to say 'No, No, No,' before marriage, it is hard for some to say 'Yes! Yes! Yes!' after marriage."

Remember the study I pointed to earlier that showed that the single highest predictor of teenage girls' remaining chaste was the girls' participation in team sports? At first blush, team sports and sexual abstinence seem to have nothing to do with each other. But in fact, the relationship makes sense: through soccer and tennis and field hockey, those girls are learning how to inhabit their bodies in good, robustly physical ways. They are seeing their bodies change and excel and face challenges and, sometimes, fail them. Their sports teams are communities that are teaching them how to live—not as sex objects, but as bodies that are graceful and disciplined and strong. They are learning, through those tennis matches and lacrosse games, that their bodies should be celebrated, because their bodies do great things.

This doesn't mean, of course, that if only the church sponsored more softball leagues, everyone would stay on the chaste straight and narrow. But it does mean that the church ought to cultivate ways of teaching Christians to live in their bodies well—so that unmarried folks can still be bodily people, even though they're not having sex, and so that married people can give themselves to sex freely.

You've Come a Long Way, Baby: From Gnosticism to Technique

If a recent Valentine's Day display at my local Christian bookstore is any indicator, Christian publishing is making great strides toward affirming that people's bodies are great because they can do great things. Lined up on a table draped with red crepe paper was a medley of recent Christian sex guides. The books—with titles like *Intimate Issues* and *A Celebration of Sex*—were all written for married people, of course, but otherwise they weren't that different from the sex guides you could find at Barnes & Noble.

These books are twenty-first-century riffs on a theme first articulated by Marabel Morgan, whose 1973 bestseller *The Total Woman* urged wives to greet their husbands clad only in Saran Wrap. In 1975, James Dobson followed with *What Wives Wish Their Husbands Knew About Women*, and the next year Tim and Beverly LaHaye came out with *The Act of Marriage*.

Books like *Intimate Issues* tell us a lot about how the church is thinking about sex these days. They tell us that sex is a "beautiful gift" from God, that He wants married couples to find sex "erotic, fulfilling, free, and beautiful." Orgasms, if not the main goal of sex, are "the frosting on the cake," and "because the frosting is so tasty, it bears further investigation." (Did you know that women are more likely to have orgasms if they exercise a lot?) Vibrators are OK with God, as are quickies. One book lays out three different types of sex—hors d'oeuvre sex ("it satisfies and whets the appetite for a good, regular meal"), home-cooked sex (fifteen minutes to a half-hour of "warmth, foreplay, and intercourse"), and gourmet sex ("long, lazy, luxurious romance with no responsibility except loving");

husbands and wives are encouraged to plan at least one round of gourmet sex a month.

Apparently the books are working. A 1994 study by researchers at the University of Chicago determined that conservative Protestant women have more orgasms than women of any other religious stripe, with 32 percent claiming to have an orgasm every time they have sex. (Mainline Protestants and Catholics clocked in at 27 percent, those with no religious affiliation at 22 percent.) At least in some Christian bookstores—and bedrooms—we've come a long way from the gnostic heresy.

I, for one, applaud. I think it's fantastic that Christians are able to embrace—indeed, pursue—bodily pleasure and the unique ecstasy of sex. I bought a copy of *Intimate Issues* and sent it to Suzanne. In translating *The Joy of Sex* into a Christian idiom, we have vigorously affirmed the goodness of married sex.

But have we also begun to parrot a story that says sex is always supposed to be exciting, that defines good sex by the frequency of the orgasm? Advice columnists and sex therapists respond with 7 tips to rekindle desire, 8 steps to a sizzling marriage bed, 9 tricks for "boosting your marriage libido."

Secular culture, after all, has made a fetish of sexual technique, suggesting that if we just follow the steamy tips of experts, sex will be frequent, and always a fantastic production that culminates in astonishing multiple orgasms. This is the message that creeps into our e-mail inboxes in the seemingly incessant unsolicited ads for potions, pills, and devices that will "increase sexual performance" (itself a disturbing phrase suggesting that sex is a theatrical production to be enacted according to the dictates of a director, a play cloaked in costumes and props). *Glamour* fills readers in on "11 Sex Moves Men Wish You'd Make" and "9 Sex Moves Men Wish You'd Skip." In a recent issue of *Maxim*, I saw an ad hawking a pillow designed to promote a greater variety of sexual positions; the pillow, tellingly, is called The Liberator. It is meant, I suppose, to liberate us from the natural constraints of our limbs and mattresses. And on and on. According to books like *The Sex-Starved Marriage* (and according to shopworn jokes about marriage being the great guarantor of chastity), married couples are in an outright crisis of libido. Twenty percent of married couples have sex less than once a month. Couples are harried, busy, stressed, exhausted. They're clinically depressed, or their hormones are out of whack, or they're dealing with childhood sexual abuse. Whatever the cause, married folks don't seem to be having much sex.

To be sure, one hopes that satisfying sex characterizes the majority of American marriages. But the tips and steps and easy how-tos for married folk seem to misdiagnose the problem. The problem is not only that new moms are exhausted and collapse into bed at night wanting only sleep. The problem is also that we think we need to aspire to Hollywood sex; we think husbands and wives, when they're doing it right, will approximate the unbridled passion of Halle Berry and Billy Bob Thornton in *Monster's Ball*. We've defined sex as something unsustainable—bodice-ripping, stupefying, and nightly. It is not only insatiable, it creates the desire for more sex. It is adventurous, not habitual, and happens best during romantic weekend getaways, after candlelit dinners that recall the restaurants you frequented on dates before you were married, before you were plunged into routine.

Good sex, to be sure, is characterized by physical pleasure. It is also conditioned by moral context. And, as I suggested in the last chapter, it is inextricable from domestic routine. Moms and dads do need to be intentional about making time for sex, but Christians can perhaps remind the broader culture that good sex, by definition, is part and parcel of, not antagonistic to, ordinary marriages and domestic life.

Catholic novelist Walker Percy often took latter-day Gnosticism as his theme. He suggested that our failure to live well in our bodies manifests itself in two ways (manifestations that may be in tension with one another, but that are not mutually exclusive). Either we live as angels, as though we don't have bodies, or we live as beasts, as if bodies are all there is. In either scenario, we witness the "trivialization of the erotic by its demotion to yet another technique and need satisfaction of the organism."

It can seem that we are left to navigate an apparent Scylla and Charybdis. We Christians don't want to—cannot—accept the culture's story about sex: that sex is only for fun, that sex has no consequences, that what I do with my body is none of your business, that the goodness of sex is evaluated by the mind-blowingness of the orgasm. But nor ought we err on the side of a Gnosticism that tells us that sexual desire is bad, that bodily longings are to be stamped out of existence. Neither of these is the Christian approach, for the Christian approach is neither hedonism nor obliteration; it is discipline.

Part Two

PRACTICING CHASTITY

6

ON THE STEPS
OF THE ROTUNDA

Line-Drawing and Formation

Legalism fails miserably at the one thing it is supposed to do: encourage obedience.

—Philip Yancey

A story about my friend Marla: Marla recently came back to Charlottesville for a long holiday with her family. While here, she reconnected with an old friend from high school, someone she hadn't seen in almost a decade. They ran into each other on the Downtown Mall, made small talk, exchanged e-mail addresses. Josh e-mailed Marla: did she want to meet for coffee? The next afternoon, they drank lattes at Greenberry's. Totally innocent.

Three nights later they went to a movie. This was slightly harder to call. It was a weekend, and it was night—all signs pointing in the direction of a date. On the other hand, if there was any sexual tension, Marla was blissfully ignorant of it, and Josh wasn't giving off any indication that he was, you know, interested.

Then there followed a third outing, definitely a date: dinner at a nice restaurant, followed by watching a video at Josh's apartment. After the movie, Marla and Josh began to kiss. They kissed a lot, though Marla swears that was all they did—no tugging at her brassiere, no unzipping of jeans. But it got late, and she was sleepy, and she and Josh liked being close to each other, after all; so after all that kissing she spent the night at his place. The next morning they made scrambled eggs and told tall tales about the high-school orchestra they'd both played in, ten years before. And that afternoon, Marla called me. She was excited—she really liked Josh—but she was also a little sheepish and nervous. Marla is a pretty new Christian, and she's not sure how to draw sexual lines. She told me about her evening with Josh, and then she said, "So I want to know two things. Do you think I should go out with him again? And do you think I sinned?"

Those two questions reveal a lot about how contemporary Christians navigate the terrain of chastity. First, they make clear the sad context in which contemporary society places us—Marla wasn't certain she wanted to see Josh again, yet she had just spent the night with him. Second, Marla makes clear that Christians who are trying to live chastely want some concrete guidance. What's licit and what's illicit? What's OK and what's sinful? What's allowed and what's forbidden?

What I said to Marla was this (I was merely quoting insightful words an older friend said to me several years before): "I'm not sure," I said, "that the question you should be asking is *At what point, precisely, did I sin?* You may want to be asking if your behavior was prudent, loving, or wise. You may want to ask at what point you loved your neighbor." (Theologian Christopher West puts the question this way: "Is this . . . behavior an authentic sign of Christ's love, or is it not?")

Perhaps you can accuse me of being evasive. Part of me was tempted to tick off Marla's activities: I don't think kissing him was a sin, no; and sleeping in the same bed with him? Also,

I think, not on a par with genital intercourse, gossip, failure to tithe—and yet also not a great idea, not especially prudent, not especially loving.

This is what we want to know: we want to know where to draw the line. We know sex is out. We think that holding hands is probably pretty innocent. But we also know that there is a wide world between holding hands and having sex, lots of things our bodies might do that we must think through and pray through, embrace or avoid, flirt with or run from. We bend over backward not to sound *legalistic*, to emphasize that chastity is freedom found in restraint, to insist that chastity is far more than just a list of *dos* and *don'ts*. And that is all well and good, but we still want to know what's allowed. We want to know how to make our way.

This desire for guidance, for clarity, for some concrete help in navigating the physical side of dating relationships has presented itself every time I have spoken to a group of college students or twenty- and thirty-somethings about sex. We panelists will talk at great length about the biblical view of sex. We will talk about the beauty of chastity. We will critique, sometimes quite trenchantly, what "the culture" has to say about sex. And inevitably, some courageous soul in the audience will raise his hand (it's almost always a he, a fact that speaks less to men's libidos and more to women's feeling somewhat less permission to speak about sex in public) and say, "This is all well and good, but what I want to know is, what can I do with my girlfriend?"

It is appropriate for Christian communities to have those slightly uncomfortable and slightly embarrassing conversations about "where to draw the line." A somewhat extreme example will make the point. Think back to Bill Clinton and Monica Lewinsky. Clinton said, under oath, that he had not had sexual relations with Monica Lewinsky; and then, of course, we all learned that he'd had oral sex with her. When he claimed that he hadn't had sexual relations, he meant he had not engaged in genital intercourse. Turns out that many American teenagers agreed with him. Studies by academics and anecdotal evidence

by reporters suggest that many teens have oral sex, but still
proudly declare themselves "pure" and "chaste." This narrow
definition, that sex equals vaginal penetration, seems even
to be shared by many Christian teens—and why not? They
breathe the same cultural air as the rest of America. They've
grown up on television, tutored early on in the arts of parsing
and spin.

OK, readers. Does St. Paul say anything explicitly about
oral sex? No. Could one make a tortured, literalistic argument that one was having oral sex and not breaking the letter
of biblical law? I suppose so. And yet most honest and right-
thinking Christians recognize, at least intuitively, that oral
sex constitutes sex—that if a husband (such as Bill Clinton)
had oral sex with someone other than his wife, he would have
committed adultery; and that a single person's having oral sex
would constitute a trespass of chastity.

Around the time that Marla and Josh went out for dinner, I
began dating Griff. We got into the habit of taking an evening
walk on the Lawn, the architectural heart of the University
of Virginia. We usually began our walks by the dome-shaped
Rotunda and ended up at Cabell Hall. Griff's friend Greg, a
campus pastor at the University of Virginia, sized up the situation and gave us this piece of guidance: "Don't do anything
sexual that you wouldn't be comfortable doing on the steps of
the Rotunda." (This was not just practical instruction, but also
wisdom: sex has a public dimension and a private dimension.
Christians gain access to the private side at a wedding. The
question for unmarried couples is not *How far can we go?* but
*How do we maintain the integrity of our sexual relationship,
which at this point is only public?*)

Griff and I took Greg's words to heart. We even climbed
up on the Rotunda's steps one night, and kissed to our hearts'
content—and then said, "Well, that's it, there's our line. We
don't really feel comfortable stripping our clothes off up here
in front of the Rotunda." And that became our mantra: on the
steps of the Rotunda. Other people have suggested a paternal
guideline—only touch your beau the way you would touch

him if your father were in the room. But that image is a little too Freudian, overdetermined, and weird for me. I prefer to picture the grounds of the University of Virginia.

I realize some readers will think that kissing ought to be off limits until you've said I do. If you're in the no-kissing camp, don't worry, I won't try to talk you out of it. I know people who've held to the no-kissing-before-marriage rule, and through knowing them I've moved from thinking they're nuts to having the utmost respect for them. But I never joined their cause. What's compelling about the no-kissing rule is its clarity. It is very, very clear. It admits no gray area. If you're not even smooching, you're unlikely to find yourself sliding down a slippery slope to sex itself. There is something decidedly unnatural about sparking desire and then arresting it, night after night. To refrain from kissing is to avoid not only temptation, but also the odd shocks, fits, and starts of interrupted desire.

But there is something in the anti-kissing stance that I find worrisome.

I am wary of dating relationships in which no physical attraction is ever expressed. I see the sense of not going too far, of not tempting fate (or Satan). But there are also real dangers in the wholesale denial of physical affection. The problem is not so much "repression"—the term secular critics of Christianity have thrown at Christian sexual ethics for at least fifty years—rather it is our old friend Gnosticism. God created us with bodies and we are meant to inhabit them. Denying any physical expression of love seems to me to edge toward the Gnostic.

The point is not that you should visit Charlottesville, kiss your sweetie on the steps of the Rotunda, and draw your line there. Rather the point is to discern, with your community, what behaviors can protect the body and God's created sexual intent. And I would underscore—by now this will come as no surprise—the role of community. One of the reasons Griff and I felt comfortable with the Rotunda rule was that we trusted its source—a slightly older, very married pastor, used to working with college students and twenty-somethings. Also, Greg was someone who knew Griff very well, one of Griff's first friends in Charlottesville. I don't know if Greg offers that Rotunda rule to everyone he counsels. I do know that he was familiar with the particularities of Griff's and my sexual backgrounds. And he used those particularities in helping us set a guideline that could both introduce Griff (who not only was a virgin but had only ever been kissed once, and that was seven years ago) to physical intimacy, and help keep me on the straight and narrow. It felt a little weird, at times, having our sexual boundaries on display before our friends. But in so doing, we were reminded that we were participating in a holy discipline, not making an individual choice. We were encouraged, even blessed. We were treated to accountability, and transparency, and good, honest conversation partners.

Griff and I both learned a few good things with our on-the-steps-of-the-Rotunda kissing. The Rotunda rule established in us a certain discipline—and perhaps a little disciplined sexuality might itself be good preparation for marriage, for the week when your wife has a urinary tract infection, or the few months after your husband's father dies, and sex is not in the cards, but maybe some kissing is.

Our kissing also inculcated in us a certain respect for the freedom of limitations. It's a little like having a budget. My parents were always after me to budget, but I never bothered. During college, I rarely even balanced my checkbook. Then I moved to England, where I lived on a stipend of $9,000 a year. I quickly learned the art of budgeting. And in budgeting, I found a certain freedom. I no longer had a niggling concern in the back of my head when, say, I went out and bought a pricey party dress. Instead, I stuck to my budget, buying new clothes only once every three months—but when those shopping trips came, I didn't have to agonize over them. In fact, I didn't really have to think about them at all, because I'd done my thinking ahead of time when I plotted out my budget. The restraint allowed me some freedom. *Mutatis mutandis*, the same freedom of limitation obtains for the Rotunda rule. We kissed without guilt, because we knew we'd made this decision with clear heads and in conversation with others; we knew where we'd drawn our line, and we knew we were firmly to one side of it.

Finally, kissing established in us the expectation that we were to be present to one another's bodies; not unduly attentive to body parts, but present to our embodied, incarnated selves. Griff will tell you that he has never inhabited his body very well—he didn't play a lot of sports as a kid, he always felt vaguely ashamed that he wasn't quite as buff as his older brother. Kissing was something of an antidote to that, a school where he could learn that he is, in fact, a body, and his body is good. And our kisses taught him to see me as a person who is a body, too. Kissing helped me know that Griff saw me as something other than just a brainy interlocutor. There is, in other words, a way that physicality uniquely affirms us as particular people. Taken to an abstracting and objectifying extreme, of course, physicality and sexuality can do just the opposite—sex can make us feel that we are just bodies, just places where other people thoughtlessly and even anonymously act out their desires. But, rightly ordered, touch grounds us as particular persons with specific physical selves.

Also, Griff notes, kissing is fun. Fun is not all there is, but it should not be overlooked . . .

Cello Lessons

The choices we make every day—where we shop, what we do with our bodies, how we pass our time—form us. They shape the type of Christians we become. What we do matters—not because good behavior gets us into heaven, but because behavior, good and bad, creates certain expectations in us, teaches us certain lessons. This is one of the reasons we are taught to pray, even when we don't feel like it—because regular praying will establish in us the demeanor and stance of praising God.

Wendell Berry has noted that "a purposeless virtue is a contradiction in terms. . . . If a virtue has been thought a virtue long enough, it must be assumed to have practical justification." The reverse is true of sin. If doing virtue has some practical, incarnated benefit, indulging in sin not only estranges us from God on the level of abstraction; doing sin also teaches us falsehoods.

I understand sin's formation by way of the cello. I began to play the cello when I was eleven, and for years I learned a particular way to hold my cello bow. Unfortunately, the first bow hold I learned was wrong; my pinky finger was in the wrong position. My teacher and I were lax. We allowed the lousy bow hold to stick. I sawed away for half a decade with that bad bow hold, until my first teacher moved away and I began to take lessons with someone else. It took my new teacher three years to teach me how to correctly hold a cello bow, and for years after that, I found my old hold creeping back in. Now, finally, when I pick up a cello bow, there's barely a trace of the old contortions; but they stuck for a very, very long time.

Those cello lessons are not unlike the lessons of sin. Sin's consequences are real. Insistent sinning fixes our hearts ever faster in the same twists and distortions that were ushered in at the fall. And nowhere is this truer than with sex. Thus, a key question to ask when parsing different sexual acts is the question of formation—what expectations and habits does a given sexual behavior form in us? To use the Book of Common Prayer's phrase, what does it teach "our selves, our souls and bodies," about being creatures before God, about what sex is and what it does? These questions might lead some people to kiss, and others not to. It's hard to see that they would lead anyone to premarital fellatio.

But the question of formation is useful not only in discerning what's forbidden and what's allowed for unmarried Christians. It also helps explain some of the sexual disorders that plague married and unmarried Christians alike.

Pornography: It Teaches You That Real Bodies Aren't Good Enough

There has been a great buzz in recent years about pornography. Though porn has been with us since the eighteenth century, its new incarnation on the Internet ("I-porn," to those in the know) is luring a new, larger, and more diverse consumer base. Porn marketers used to think that their clientele was almost entirely male. But since the advent of I-porn, more women are using pornography. The trend, sociologists have suggested, has to do with social control. Women might be embarrassed to walk into an "adult bookstore" and purchase a pornographic magazine, but they can surf pornographic websites in the privacy of their own home. So too with pastors, once not thought of as a large market for pornography. The privacy and lack of accountability that draw women to I-porn seem to be attracting a growing number of ministers as well: one survey suggests that 7 percent of married clergy regularly use Internet porn; another study, conducted in 2000, found that 40 percent of clergy admit to having surfed a porn site at least once. Recall the scandal at Harvard Divinity School when, in the fall of 1998, the school's dean was forced to resign after thousands of pornographic pictures were found on his school computer. One pastor's wife recently called Focus on the Family's pastoral care hotline to report that her husband had been on a porn site not three minutes before he climbed into the pulpit Sunday morning.

Even those of us who would never Google an X-rated website or purchase *Penthouse* or *Playboy* have to be thoughtful about pornography. I used to think those folks who worried about nudity and sexual poses in magazine ads and on TV were old fuddy-duddies, but I've become persuaded of their point. Perhaps I've become an old fuddy-duddy myself, but I feel depressed when I pick up a copy of *Maxim*; I fail to see the difference between the voluptuous and scantily clad model who decorated their January 2004 cover and a shot that might grace the cover of a straight-up porn mag. It's no wonder that fraternity houses have canceled their subscriptions to *Playboy* and opted instead for the free and ubiquitous Victoria's Secret catalog—a rag that actually leaves quite little a secret. One does not have to revile above-the-knee skirts to cheer when the forces of decency win an occasional battle, as they did at the end of 2003 when, under fierce pressure from an unlikely confederation of feminist activists and Christian pundits, Abercrombie and Fitch withdrew from circulation a catalog that featured bare-breasted young women performing unabashedly sexual deeds to smiling young men. (You'd think that a clothing company might prefer a catalog filled with models wearing clothes.)

Porn turns sex into something simultaneously fantastic and exploitative, removing it from the relational reality of marriage, importing outside standards into the bedroom, and thereby objectifying whatever living and breathing fleshly person one might later have sex with. Pornography is destructive because it communicates a tacit narrative about physical gratification without saying a thing about how sex really happens. It teaches its clientele expectations that are, simply, not connected to reality, to real men and women with real bodies (not to mention real souls, hearts, and minds).

This is well illustrated by a scene in Clyde Edgerton's novel *Raney*. The year is 1975. Raney is a small-town Southern Baptist married to Charles, a more liberal Christian from Atlanta. Throughout the novel, Edgerton manages to poke fun at, and be sympathetic to, both Raney and Charles, but in the relevant scene, Raney has the clear upper hand. Raney has caught Charles buying a copy of *Penthouse*. Understandably, Raney freaks. And then Charles goes ballistic, insisting that what he reads is none of her business: "We happen to be living in a free country which tells me in its own constitution that I am free to read what I want to . . . without reporting in to you." He then suggests that Raney could "pick up a few pointers" from *Penthouse*. Raney is no sophisticate. She hasn't taken college classes in spiritual formation, much less feminist theory. But she understands the power of pornography. "How am I supposed to carry on a normal sex life with somebody who is reading these filthy magazines and coming up with no telling what in his mind," she demands.

The scene from *Raney* has its parallels in real life, too. In a *New York* magazine article about the rise of Internet porn, David Amsden reports that "recently, a 26-year-old businessman friend shocked me by casually remarking, 'Dude, all of my friends are so obsessed with Internet porn that they can't sleep with their girlfriends unless they act like porn stars.'" Feminist critic Naomi Wolf makes the same point: "The onslaught of porn is responsible for deadening male libido in relation to real women," she writes. "For most of human history, erotic images have been reflections of, or celebrations of, or substitutes for, real naked women. For the first time in human history, the images' power and allure have supplanted that of real naked women. Today, real naked women are just bad porn."

Pornography, which teaches us to look at people abstracted from family, job, and context, offers an exclusively sexual category for another person. Clyde Edgerton's Charles doesn't think of the pin-ups as people; the *Penthouse* models become for Charles, non-people, mere sexuality. And porn encourages a subterranean sexual individualism; to wit Charles's protestations that if he wants to read *Penthouse*, that's his business, not his wife's. The individualism of pornography, of course, is linked to that other autoerotic activity—masturbation.

Masturbation: It Teaches You that Sex Happens Outside a Relationship

At 6:30 every Tuesday morning, a group of ten or so men meet at a well-appointed apartment in Boston. Three hours later, most of them will be sitting in cubicles and offices in law firms and consulting groups; one will be showing a town house in Beacon Hill, and another will be heading to Harvard Law School for a ten a.m. torts class. But for these early morning hours, they pray and study the Bible and share their struggles and hopes for the week ahead. Tom, the man in whose apartment they meet, has been getting together with this group of guys for over five years now. He always makes coffee; someone else brings donuts. If you get Tom talking about the group, he will tell you it is a touchstone. "It's where we get our batteries recharged," he says. "It's a place we can let down our guard and be real with each other, as Christian men trying to live out the gospel."

He will also tell you that his crew spends at least thirty minutes of their weekly morning meeting discussing masturbation. "It's one of the things we really struggle with, there's no doubt about that," says Tom.

Tom and his buddies are not alone. Throw a stone at a group of Christian young adults, and you're likely to hit someone who is puzzling through the topic of masturbation: *Is it right or wrong? How do I break the habit? What's going on emotionally when I masturbate? Why is this such a big deal, anyway?*

Christians today know that the myths of our grandparents' generation—that masturbation will make you blind, or will cause you to grow green hair all over your hands—are untrue. But myths about masturbation do sometimes still circulate in Christian circles, most significantly an inaccurate retelling of the biblical story of Onan. Onan's name, actually, is the etymological root of an old-fashioned term for masturbation, *onanism*. That term attests to a persistent misunderstanding of the story.

We meet Onan in Genesis 38. The son of Judah, Onan had an older brother named Er. Er married Tamar, but died before they had children. In the custom of the day, it was Onan's obligation to marry Tamar and father her children—but the offspring would carry on the line of his dead brother, not the line of Onan himself. Onan was having no part of it. He married Tamar, but "Onan knew that the offspring would not be his; so whenever he lay with his brother's wife, he spilled his semen on the ground to keep from producing offspring for his brother. What he did was wicked in the Lord's sight; so he put him to death."

For centuries Christian moralists have misinterpreted—arguably, deliberately misconstrued—this tale, stating in tract and sermon that Onan was punished because he masturbated. But all biblical scholars agree that this is plainly not the case. Onan was punished because he refused to fulfill Hebraic law and father children on behalf of his brother. It was this, and not the act of "spilling his semen" that "was wicked in the Lord's sight." He could have simply refused to sleep with Tamar. The outcome would have been the same: the Lord would still have been angry and struck Onan down.

All that to say that the Bible does not say anything about masturbation per se. The story about Onan, though often glossed as a tale about the evils of autoeroticism, does not, in fact, tell us whether masturbation is right or wrong; it tells us only that it is wrong to try to avoid fathering your brother's children if your brother has left a childless widow.

Scripture doesn't come out and say "don't masturbate," nor does it say "Go for it!" As Christian columnist Tim Stafford notes, "Masturbation is difficult to put in a good-or-evil category. . . . The Bible isn't shy about mentioning sex, but masturbation is never referred to. I think the very least you can conclude is that masturbation isn't the most important issue in the world from God's perspective." So we are left with a gray area. Are there principles in scripture that lead us to a clear rejection of masturbation? Or that allow us to enthusiastically encourage it?

Some Christian ethicists, in their counsel about masturbation, have drawn gender distinctions. The mechanics of the male orgasm are pretty straightforward. Women's physiology is a bit more complicated, and lots of women are not sure what an orgasm feels like, or how to have one. (Indeed, the exact workings of women's orgasms—what precisely causes them, where they happen, and how necessary or helpful genital intercourse is in producing them—continue to be topics of debate among gynecologists, feminists, Freudians, and ordinary women themselves.) One pastor I know told me he doesn't have a blanket rule on masturbation. "Unmarried men," he said, "are either going to masturbate or have wet dreams, because the sperm has to get out somehow. So occasional—not habitual, but occasional—masturbation is probably OK. But I would urge a married man not to masturbate—for to do so would really be an act of infidelity to his wife." For women, this pastor reverses things. "Many married women," he says, "especially but not exclusively newly married women, may need to spend some time figuring their own bodies out," if only so that they can figure out what they like and how they like it—and then teach their husbands how to make them feel good.

I used to be very much of the school that thought Christians were way too anxious about masturbation. I thought masturbation probably was not a very big deal, that God probably didn't care one way or the other. And I am still perplexed by the energy some unmarried Christians pour into avoiding masturbation. In erring on the side of purity, as it were, we seem to have created a culture of profound anxiety, which itself can form us in a distorted sexuality. Newly married men who have spent their teens and twenties wrestling with masturbation often spend the first few years of their marriage wrestling with sexual pleasure. If a man spends ten or fifteen premarital years teaching himself that sexual pleasure is bad and ought to induce guilt, he's not usually able to wave a magic wand on his wedding night and experience his wife's hands as instruments of guilt-free goodness.

But if an overly strict avoidance of masturbation can leave us skittish about even rightly ordered sexual pleasure, frequent masturbation can also form us in strange and false understandings of sexuality—not least the idea that sexual pleasure is an individual, and individualistic, undertaking. Masturbation teaches us that immediate gratification is a part of sex, and masturbation removes sex from a relationship. Indeed, the whole point of masturbation is to provide the release and pleasure of orgasm without the work and joy of a relationship.

Masturbating is almost always coupled with fantasizing, as evidenced by this heartfelt defense of masturbation by Doug Roberts, a contributor to *Glamour*: "[O]ne of the things I love about masturbation is that it's sex with anybody I want: Halle Berry, the weather-woman, the blond who brushed against me on the subway. . . . I can summon any one (or two) of these ladies for a romp under the covers. Or on the kitchen table. Or in an Exxon station bathroom, for that matter. Why not be adventurous? It's not as if she'll balk at the idea. . . . Ah, the freedom of solo sex. When you don't have somebody else's wants and needs to consider, you can have whatever experience you'd like." A paean to the glories of unfettered individualism and straightforward selfishness!

It is here that masturbating plunges us into a world of unreality. For the weather-woman or the cute guy from work is not thinking about you. In this way, masturbation can be closely linked to pornography: in the same *New York* magazine article I mentioned above, we meet a guy named Rick, a good-looking twenty-something who likes women, really wants to date, but is intimidated by the women he meets. "Girls . . . are waiting for . . . a movie star, or a 50-year-old guy to be their sugar daddy," says Rick. "They want someone . . . who lives on Fifth Avenue—not someone who lives in Williamsburg with two other dudes." Rick's solution is to masturbate to I-porn. "Thing is, you can find a million girls just like them online," he says. "And they're naked, doing whatever you want them to do." This is, in Rick's own astute phrase, a "substitute for reality."

Think about the guy who dials a 900 number and masturbates during phone sex. Your phone-sex lady may be talking passionate talk; she may be saying that she wants you; but in reality *she doesn't know who you are*. That a sexual act serves as a "substitute for reality" ought to give us pause. After all, we Christians are the people devoted to living the really real.

The Elephant in the Room: Safeguarding Marital Sexuality

Consider the phrase *premarital sex*. Premarital sex itself is a bad thing, but the phrase is a good one. It asserts, unabashedly, that there is some connection between marriage and sex. It implies that marital sex is the norm and premarital sex a deviation—"sex," unadorned by adjective, would imply "marital," so we need a distinctive phrase for denoting sex before marriage. It is surprising that in a place and time where sex has become so thoroughly unyoked from marriage the usage has been retained. It seems almost quaint.

But marriage remains the standard-bearer. Though it is sometimes annoying, and sometimes downright painful for single people to constantly hold marriage in the back of their heads, marriage must be part of any conversation about Christian sexuality, for in a Christian moral grammar, marriage is the only context for sex. Therefore, when we think about premarital sexuality, we always have to name the elephant in the room: marital sexuality. Licit, good premarital sexual behavior safeguards and protects marital sexuality. I'd say, for instance, that in our Rotunda osculation, Griff and I learned lessons that would stand both of us in good stead down the road in marriage. Not so with masturbating. The immediate gratification of masturbation is simply not a characteristic of married sex, for marriage requires coordinating and immersing your desires in a dynamic relationship. In masturbation, you control your sex life; marital sex requires the surrender of control to another person.

Indeed, safeguarding marital sexuality is one way that premarital chastity is active and positive. To be premaritally chaste is not to sit passively by and simply avoid sex; it is to participate in an active protection of a created good. This is part of how we answer Marla's question about what's allowed and what's forbidden: we call something off-limits if it establishes habits and expectations that may ultimately prove destructive to marital sexuality. And premarital sex itself—even premarital sex between two people who love each other—forms us in false sexual habits, habits that ultimately do violence to marital sex.

Premarital Sex: It Teaches You that Sex Is Thrilling

The main story our society tells about non-marital sex is that it's exciting. Indeed, "exciting" and "thrilling" are among the adjectives our popular culture most frequently attaches to sex. And premarital sex can be exciting. Folks who are in the dating pool cannot assume they are going to have sex every night, or every week. Sex isn't regular. It isn't ordinary. To the contrary, it is *dramatic*. Sometimes it is dramatic because it is bound up with the thrill of the chase—this is the drama of the much-touted college "hook-up." You get all gussied up and go to a party and you have a goal: to attract that cute man with the long eyelashes. Flirting is exciting. Knowing someone finds you attractive feels good. Not knowing the outcome—*Will he or won't he? Does she or doesn't she?*—can be thrilling.

Sometimes premarital sex feels dramatic because, by definition, it is part of a relationship that is itself not wholly stable. Even when you've been dating someone for a year, the lack of permanence that fundamentally characterizes your relationship can add a certain frisson to everything you do with that person, from going on a Saturday hike to smooching on the sofa. Everything in your relationship gets some of its charge from the uncertainty, the unknown: put negatively, it gets its charge from the instability; put more generously, it gets its charge from the possibility.

This may be the single most significant way that married sex differs from unmarried sex. Married sex does not derive its thrill from the possibility of the unknown. Married sex is a given. It is solemnized and marked in ritual. It is established. It is governed by vows. It becomes a ritual in itself; it becomes a routine.

The sex of blind dates and fraternity parties, even of relatively long-standing dating relationships, has, simply, no normal qualities. Based principally on mutual desire, it dispenses with the ordinary rhythms of marital sex, trading them for a seemingly thrilling but ultimately false story. This may be the way that the sin of premarital sex sticks with us most lastingly; it may be the twisted lesson it teaches us most convincingly: that sex is exciting. That sex derives its thrill from instability and drama. In fact, the opposite is true: the dramas of married sex are smaller and more intimate, and indeed it is the stability of marriage that allows sex to be what it is.

Think this mind-set has no consequences on marriages? Just surf the web to an online dating service and keep your eye out for married users—yes, married men and women who admit they're married and say they're simply looking for a little exciting sex on the side. ("I'm 33, live in midtown, work downtown for a major financial house in risk management, married, no kids. Been cheating almost since I got married. With the various women I've been with, it's ranged from straight vanilla sex to . . . making a home movie.")

If the predictability of married sex doesn't drive everyone to place an adulterous personal ad, many married couples do complain about the difference between the exhilarating sex they had as singles and the routine sex they're having with their spouse. Magazines are full of advice columns trying to foster "excitement" and "spontaneity" in married couples' workaday sexual routines. The excitement needs to be fostered because it has come to be expected: newlyweds used to the thrills of the dating scene often speak of disillusionment, a headachy dullness that sets in when they realize that married sex, whatever else it may be, is habitual.

There's nothing inherently wrong with married couples fostering a little romance. There's nothing wrong with the husband who buys his wife some lingerie or lights a few candles in the bedroom. The problem comes before that—it comes in a set of premarital sexual experiences that foster the expectation that sex will be constantly exciting, that it will be thrilling the way instability is almost always thrilling, the way walking on a rope bridge across a gorge can be thrilling. The problem comes when we learn to define excitement by instability's terms, to connect sexuality and desire with that instability, instead of teaching us to find it in the stable, daily—and yes, occasionally dull—rhythms of marriage.

The unique delights of married sex are described well by Alexandra Marshall in her novel *The Court of Common Pleas*. Her protagonists are Gregory and Audrey, a restrained, middle-aged couple living in Ohio. They've been married for twenty years, and when our novel starts, they have a fight. A big fight; a fight that threatens to undo their marriage.

But they speak, and they shower, and they have sex.

And now it was an advantage that Gregory had come of age in the generation that contented itself with being good. Audrey was in no danger of being overwhelmed by a lust encrusted with the aspects of a performance. . . . 'Comfort food,' they called this function of lovemaking, not because it was bland but because, like meatloaf and mashed potatoes, macaroni and cheese, their associations enlarged the experience. He could know that she would rake her fingers though his hair like a fork, pulling it straight back to expose the subtly off-center V-shaped point his mother gave him . . . as a widow's peak. Audrey could know he would cater to her and sense whether she was feeling patient or impatient.

Like macaroni and cheese, this married lovemaking was not especially surprising, not particularly exotic, but very satisfying.

The problem comes when the "thrills" and "excitement" of premarital sex unfit us for the comfort and knowledge of Gregory and Audrey's sex.

That people have sex outside marriage is understandable; we fornicate for the same reason we practice idolatry. Idolatry carries in it the seed of a good impulse—the impulse to worship our Maker. Idolatry is that good impulse wrongly directed to disastrous ends. Like idolatry, fornication is a wrong reflection of a right creational impulse. We were made for sex. And so premarital sex tells a partial truth; that's why it resonates with something. But partial truths are destructive. They push us to created goods wrongly lived. To borrow a phrase from Thomas Cranmer again: they are ultimately destructive to our selves, our souls and bodies.

7

CHASTITY
AS SPIRITUAL DISCIPLINE

Conforming Your Body to the Arc of the Gospel

Chastity makes us familiar with God.

—John Climacus

Let's get down to brass tacks. What is chastity? One way of putting it is that chastity is doing sex in the Body of Christ—doing sex in a way that befits the Body of Christ, and that keeps you grounded, and bounded, in the community. As we've seen, that means sex only within marriage—which means, in turn, abstinence if you're not married, and fidelity if you are.

Sex is, in Paul's image, a joining of your body to someone else's. In baptism, you have become Christ's Body, and it is Christ's Body that must give you permission to join His Body to another body. In the Christian grammar, we have no *right* to sex. The place where the church confers that privilege on you is the wedding; weddings grant us license to have sex with one person. Chastity, in other words, is a fact of gospel life. In the New Testament, sex beyond the boundaries of marriage—the boundaries of communally granted sanction of sex—is simply off limits. To have sex outside those bounds is to commit an offense against the Body. Abstinence before marriage, and fidelity within marriage; any other kind of sex is embodied apostasy.

So Do We Just Have to Grit Our Teeth and Bear It?

Chastity, then, is a basic rule of the community, but it is not a mere rule. It is also a discipline.

The language of spiritual discipline, an ancient idiom of the church, has come into vogue again. In the 1970s and '80s, two books on spiritual disciplines, now rightly considered modern-day classics, were published: Richard Foster's *Celebration of Discipline* and Dallas Willard's *The Spirit of the Disciplines*. Foster and Willard called readers to deepen their Christian lives by incorporating ancient practices of the church. These books struck a tremendous chord, and Christians of all stripes began exploring habits and structures like liturgical prayer, fasting, solitude, simplicity, and tithing.

The spiritual disciplines are things that we do; they are things that we practice. They are ways we orient our whole selves—our bodies and minds and hearts, our communities and rhythms and ways of being in the world—toward God. Thinking of spirituality as something we practice or do strikes some people as odd—isn't the point of Christianity that Jesus saves you regardless of what you do? Sure. Doing spiritual practices doesn't get you into heaven. Rather, practicing spiritual disciplines helps align your feelings, your will, and your habits with God's will.

Discipline is a modern term for what the old church would have called "asceticism," which comes from the Latin word *ascesis*, which means exercise. And, indeed, the spiritual disciplines are, in part, exercises that train us in the Christian life. Thinking about physical exercise, actually, can help us understand spiritual exercise. Serious runners run at least three or four times a week, rain or shine, whether or not they feel like it. Even on the days you don't enjoy your jogs, you know that you are maintaining your skills and strengths so that you can go for that run on the beach when you want to. Spiritual practices form in us the habits, skills, and strengths of faithful followers of Christ. Committing myself to a discipline of daily prayer, for example, teaches me how to be a person of prayer. Committing myself to tithing, even when it pinches my budget, turns me into a person who understands that all is a gift, that all belongs to God. As Willard explains in *The Spirit of the Disciplines*, spiritual practices "mold and shape" us. They are activities "undertaken to bring us into more effective cooperation with Christ and his Kingdom. . . . To grow in grace is to grow in what is given to us of God and by God. The disciplines are then, in the clearest sense, a means to that grace and also to those gifts."

Some ancient spiritual practices may feel awkward and foreign—like keeping a vigil. "Keeping vigil" is just poetic church-speak for staying up all night in prayer. I first tried to keep a vigil several years ago, when I lived in England. A group of us had decided to hold a special vigil to pray for an upcoming meeting of Anglican bishops, and our plan seemed simple enough. We would simply stay awake, and praying, from nine o'clock at night until the seven o'clock prayer service the next morning. We even scheduled breaks for coffee and croissants.

I found vigil-keeping incredibly difficult. By two a.m., I was flat-out exhausted and wanted nothing more than a catnap. I couldn't understand what good this vigil was doing, and I began to doubt that Jesus really cared whether I stayed at it. Weren't my prayers just as valuable at four in the afternoon as at four in the morning? But as I began to doze off, God visited me with the grace of remembering scripture. In the beginnings of sleep, I could picture Jesus climbing out of the Garden of Gethsemane and finding his disciples, whom he'd asked to stay awake with him, dozing; and I could hear Jesus asking, "Could you not stay awake one hour?"

Chastity as Spiritual Discipline: Or, What Chastity Has in Common with Abstaining from Brie

Chastity, too, is a spiritual discipline. Chastity is something you do, it is something you practice. It is not only a state—the state of *being chaste*—but a disciplined, active undertaking that we *do* as part of the Body. It is not the mere absence of sex but an active conforming of one's body to the arc of the gospel.

The disciplines of Christian sexuality can be seen, too, when we look at sex between married people. Here the discipline of sex is twofold. Fidelity is a discipline: just as most single people want to have sex, period, so married people (even really happily married people) find themselves wanting to have sex with someone other than their spouse. And restraining those impulses is itself a discipline. (Indeed, it is worth pointing out that practicing chastity before you are married trains you well for chastity after you are married; it stands to reason that those who are promiscuous before marriage may be more likely to cheat on their spouses once married.) But so too is having sex with your husband or wife a discipline. Sometimes we have sex with our spouse because we feel desire, because we want to express the intimacy we feel, because we feel turned on; but sometimes a husband and wife have sex precisely because they don't feel desire or intimacy. We recognize that sex can do good work between a husband and wife, that it can do the work of rekindling that desire and intimacy, that bodies have something to teach us, and that sex is not about spirits communing, but about *persons being bodies together*.

Speaking of spiritual discipline seems to elevate chastity from gritting-my-teeth-and-stonily-avoiding-sex to something lofty, noble, and spiritual. But when I speak of chastity as a spiritual discipline, I also mean something eminently practical. Speaking of chastity as a spiritual discipline immediately connects it to the other disciplines. In the spiritual life, these disciplines cannot be severed from one another.

Prayer—fixing on one's contact and communion with God— is the bedrock discipline. All the other spiritual disciplines, like fasting and chastity, depend upon prayer and are, in fact, forms of prayer. My pastor is always reminding me that prayer and Bible study must precede, accompany, and support any other spiritual exercises.

Prayer and Bible study are basic, but I think fasting can be a good companion to chastity as well. I say this as one who is not a big fan of fasting. In fact, I began fasting only fairly recently, and only because my pastor more or less insisted. So now, once a week, I give my day over to this discipline. I drink fruit juice, but I don't eat. ("Isn't chugging V-8 Splash sort of cheating?" I asked my pastor when he first suggested protein-enriched juice might be allowed. He chuckled. "Just try it. All the juice in the world won't make you feel like you've bitten into a hamburger.") I know in advance, now, that I won't be as good a writer or teacher on the days that I fast. I know I might get headaches. I know that by late afternoon I might be short-tempered with anyone who crosses my path.

But I'm beginning to understand some of the benefits of fasting; I'm beginning to see that I recognize my dependence on God more clearly when I'm hungry; I'm beginning to chip away at some of the stupor that comes with always being sated. I've not achieved that highly evolved state where I look forward to it. I wish there were an easier, less annoying way to reap the fruits of fasting, but I don't think there is. What fasting is slowly teaching me is the simple lesson that I am not utterly subject to my bodily desires. I'll admit here that cheese is my favorite food. I especially like sharp white cheddar cheese. I would eat it at every meal if I could. One day I realized I'd done just that; I had eaten cheese at the last six meals. So I decided I'd take just three days off, eat no cheese until Thursday (when I had plans to meet a friend at the pizza parlor). This seemingly small gustatory sacrifice was a mini-revelation. On Tuesday, for example, I found myself at a cafeteria for lunch, and there was yummy looking mac and cheese. The world would not have ended if I'd eaten some. I don't think God was sitting in heaven jotting notes to Himself about my cheese intake. But in passing up the cheese, I got the inkling of a lesson—I am not captive to this desire. I can pass the mac and cheese up. I can say, *Nope, today I'm fasting from cheese.*

St. Francis of Assisi famously called his body "Brother Ass." It is fasting, I think, that helps us say to our body, You are Brother (or Sister), but you are also Ass. Fasting, in other words, is the practice that most obviously helps us learn to discipline our physical selves. A woman of the early church known as holy Syncletia taught that "bodily poison is cured by still stronger antidotes; so fasting and prayer drive sordid temptations from us." I have a happily married friend who puts that in a modern idiom. He says that when he wants to have sex with someone other than his wife, he fasts. In remembering that he can discipline his desire for food, my friend reminds himself that he can discipline his desire for sex, too.

Of course, premarital abstinence is different from fasting, because when you fast you know you will eat again. Premarital abstinence is different from keeping vigil, because during your vigil you can be confident that you will sleep again. Unmarried Christians have no guarantee that they will ever get married. They have no guarantee of licit sex. Thus to practice premarital chastity is at times to feel as if you are being forever forbidden the satisfaction of a normal appetite.

Understanding chastity as a discipline helps us quiet that nagging voice in our heads that says, "I'm being made to give up something that is totally normal and natural!" Of course, the desire for sex is normal and natural, but many spiritual disciplines—the so-called disciplines of abstinence—center on refraining from something normal. One who keeps vigil is abstaining from sleep in order to abide with God; one who fasts is abstaining from food in order to see that one is truly hungry for God; one who spends time alone forgoes the company of others in order to deepen a conversation with God; one who practices simplicity avoids luxury in order to attend more clearly to God. And the unmarried Christian who practices chastity refrains from sex in order to remember that

God desires your person, your body, more than any man or woman ever will.

With all aspects of ascetic living, one does not avoid or refrain from something for the sake of rejecting it, but for the sake of something else. In this case, one refrains from sex with someone other than one's spouse for the sake of union with Christ's Body. That union is the fruit of chastity.

Many recent proponents of modesty and chastity have pointed out that chastity can be alluring, even erotic. Dressing modestly, writes Wendy Shalit in *A Return to Modesty*, "is now what is sexy—and maybe it always was. Certainly sexual modesty may damp down superficial allure, the kind of allure that inspires a one-night stand. But the kind of allure that lasts—that is what modesty protects and inspires." According to Shalit and fellow travelers, if you are having trouble attracting the right guy, you should perhaps consider covering up a bit—trade in your miniskirts for more modest garb, and draw firm lines about physical comportment.

This argument for modest dress and behavior is almost always aimed at women. The underlying message is that quality guys are turned off, not turned on, by plunging necklines and spandex hip-huggers. I recently attended a women's retreat where one of the workshops was about singleness. The speaker, whom I'll call Myrtle, encouraged the single women in the audience to think carefully about what type of guy they were looking for. "You want a Prince Charming," Myrtle said, "and Prince Charmings are attracted to modest women. You might attract certain men by sporting skimpy skirts, but you won't attract the kind of man you really want to be with."

It's encouraging to think that mature Christians are more interested in character than cleavage; yet there is something unsettling about this assurance that chastity will be the erotic mystery that will lead Mr. Right (or Miss Right) to our door. Prince Charming can begin to rival God as the object of our attentions. Myrtle ended her talk on this note: "What we single women have to do is no more and no less than faithfully pray

that our perfect guy is out there. We don't need to hunt him
down, we just need to wait for the Lord to deliver him to us.
We don't need to worry about him. Instead we need to focus
on ourselves, becoming the type of pure, modest woman that
our Prince Charming will be on the lookout for. We need to
devote ourselves to prayer, humility, and grace. We need to
continue becoming godly women, so that, when the time is
right, we will have those godly characteristics that the godly
man we dream about will love."

I'm not disputing the desirability of the chaste woman or
man. It may well be that one of the benefits of practicing chastity is that you attract friends and admirers who admire chastity. But attracting others is not the goal of chastity. Indeed, if
Myrtle is focused on catching the eye of a guy who likes chaste
women, she may not really be inhabiting chastity at all.

Fourth-century preacher St. John Chrysostom made the
same point when teaching on a passage in Genesis. Working with the premise that not a single word of scripture is
accidental, Chrysostom asks why Genesis says, of Rebekah,
"She was a virgin, whom no man had known." Isn't that re-
dundant? Isn't a virgin, by definition, one whom no one has
know sexually? No, said Chrysostom, "It is not mere repetition
when Rebekah is called a virgin twice. . . . Many virgins keep
their bodies uncorrupted, but fill their souls with all kinds of
licentiousness. They adorn themselves, attract innumerable
admirers, and excite the eyes of young men, setting ambushes
and traps for them." Genesis's ostensible repetition shows that
Rebekah was not an ambushing tease, but "was a virgin in
both body and soul." Augustine makes the same point when,
in his commentary on Psalm 147, he says that lifelong virginity "of the flesh belongs to a few; virginity of the heart must
be the concern of all."

Myrtle seems to be working toward becoming, principally,
the kind of woman Prince Charming wants, which incidentally
may be the kind of woman God wants. Her priorities, I would
suggest, need to flip-flop. We are to become persons of God,
and this may bear the incidental fruit of attracting a great

partner. For the point of chastity is not that you turn your attention away from other people to make you more attractive to them but that you turn your attention away from sexual and romantic entanglements with other people and orient yourself toward God.

8

COMMUNITIES
OF CHASTITY

What Singleness Teaches the Church

I have community with others and I shall continue to have it only through Jesus Christ. The more genuine and the deeper our community becomes, the more will everything else between us recede, the more clearly and purely will Jesus Christ and his work become the one and only thing that is vital between us.

—Dietrich Bonhoeffer

I once brought a group of college students to a convent. We sat in on a remedial geometry class one of the sisters taught to local middle-schoolers, and we attended an evening prayer service. At the end of the day, our group had a powwow with one of the nuns, Sister Margaret. She talked a little about the history of the order and the rhythm of the nuns' weeks. She said she'd never met a sister anything like the singing mother superior in *The Sound of Music*, and then she smiled in what I thought was a very nun-like way and said, "So, now. What do you really

want to know about our life here? Ask me anything you want."
Someone asked when she knew she wanted to be a nun, and
another student asked how often she got to see her family, and
a third asked whether she was allowed to go shopping, and then
finally one bold history major from Queens asked what all of us
wanted to know: "What's the deal with not having sex?"

"I was waiting for you to ask about celibacy," Sister Margaret said, and winked. "Some people in the church, you know,
want to make some changes so that people in religious orders
no longer have to make a vow of celibacy, but I think it's an
important and good part of our life here. Not everyone is
called to this life, I know, and giving up sex is a very particular renunciation. But I think we have an easier time of it here
together in our community than you unmarried young people
do out there, alone, in the world."

Although people sometimes use the words interchangeably,
celibacy and *chastity* are not the same thing; chastity is a commitment to having sex in its proper place, whereas celibacy
is a vow of lifelong abstinence. (In the words of a celibate
religious community in New Zealand, "Celibacy is the free
choice not to be married or have sexual relations. Chastity is
the free choice to live one's sexual life in accord with Christian
values—therefore, everyone is called to live chastely.") Still, in
inhabiting chastity, Christians—married and unmarried—have
a lot to learn from celibate monks and nuns.

For monks and nuns, the practice of celibacy begins with
a vow. The men and women of religious orders come before
their community and profess celibacy to God. Their community
helps sustain their sisters and brothers in their vow. Somehow
the True Love Waits pledge cards signed in adolescence only
dimly approximate this. Perhaps the cards seem flabby because
they are so often understood as an individual pledge of the
will, and not as a promise made by and with the entire Body
of God. (Might we envision some vow taken at confirmation
that gets closer to the reality of the community's celebrating,
walking with, and supporting single people in their practice
of chastity?)

The essential insight of celibate members of religious orders is that transformation—including, but not limited to, the disciplining of sexual desires—happens in a community. Without the presence and commitment of the community, it would seem impossible for people to change; it would seem naïve to expect people to be different from their parents, or different from what their culture tells them to be. So like most spiritual disciplines, chastity is better practiced in community than alone. It is not enough for individual Christians to decide to be chaste; the church must be a community that works toward chastity, a community whose structures and rhythms make chastity seem plausible and attainable. (Here, we can take our cue not only from monasteries, but also from twelve-step groups; Alcoholics Anonymous creates a place where radical change of behavior makes sense because it creates a community. It sustains relationships that are organized around the vision of changed lives. The church, too, needs to be a community where chaste behavior makes sense, where people commit to a shared vision of lives transformed by the gospel, where transformation is expected.)

The Church: A Community for Single Christians?

More and more Americans are living single. The most recent census reported 86 million single Americans. That's a big jump from previous generations. In 1970, 36 percent of American adults were unmarried; today, the figure is 44 percent. Married couples with kids, which used to be the American norm, now constitute just 25 percent of the population, and that figure, projects the Census Bureau, will drop to 20 percent by 2010. Statisticians predict that if you live to age seventy, you'll spend more of your adult life single than married. Campaign managers and speechwriters have begun to pay attention to these demographic trends, as have marketers and advertising gurus; we'll see more and more ad copy targeting unmarried folks, and more frozen food, laundry detergent, and bottled water packaged in slender servings for singletons. If groups like the American Association for Single People have their way, tax codes and health-care benefits that seem to benefit married couples may be revised to take account of the burgeoning unmarried population.

Yet the church does not do singleness very well. Lana Trent, coauthor of *Single and Content*, has insisted that "the church doesn't realize how many people avoid services because they are too focused on families and alienate singles." Camerin Courtney, an editor for *Today's Christian Woman* and a columnist for ChristianityToday.com's singles' channel, admits that sometimes Sunday mornings are "the loneliest part of my week." It can be dispiriting to sit alone in a church seemingly full of married couples, and many single people—generally happy, well-adjusted folks—feel utterly uncomfortable in church.

Of course, part of the burden falls on single Christians themselves to transform the church into a place that welcomes all comers, and to buck a culture that insists we're not really adults until we're married. (Raise your hand if you get stuck at the kids' table over Thanksgiving while your married sibs and cousins sit with the other adults!) For me, this meant buying a nice, in fact pricey, set of pottery dishes when I was twenty-two. My mother thought I was nuts, spending what amounted to 20 percent of my student stipend on plates I was likely to break, but I wanted to prove to myself that I didn't need to be married to have decent dishes.

Still, the church needs to nurture its single people. (If only for self-interest—remember those statistics on the growing single demographic!) Despite the fact that Jesus never married, the contemporary church too often assumes that married life is the norm. Doesn't it seem that couples are always asked to light the Advent wreath and serve on important church committees? In her wonderful book *Table for One*, Camerin Courtney puzzles over the invisibility of single folks in church leadership. "In my church," she writes, "communion is served by the elders . . . often accompanied by their wives. This makes sense on logistical levels, but it leaves me with a few perplexing questions: How does being married to an elder make one more qualified to serve? . . . Will I be able to serve in this capacity only if I get married—and to someone with elder-potential? . . . I don't mean to bash the church. . . . I love the church. I *am* the church. But there are times when I feel more like its black-sheep spinster aunt than one of its valued daughters." And why is it so hard for preachers to illustrate their sermons, just occasionally, with a reference to tension between roommates instead of the challenges of marriage? (I've made myself something of a thorn in my pastor's side; every time a new church committee is convened, I e-mail to ask whether any single parishioners have been tapped to serve.)

A Community That Speaks Well about Singleness, Chastity, and Sex

We cannot help one another on the narrow road of discipleship if we can't speak truthfully with one another about the pitfalls and roadblocks we face. Communities working toward chastity ought to have honest and true conversations about sex, conversations that include opportunities for counsel and witness. All too often, the church shies away from such conversations. Four years into his marriage, my friend Mike told me that he and his now-wife had been having oral sex for about a year before they married. "I wanted to talk to my pastor about this," says Mike, "but I could never shake the suspicion that something like oral sex would be seen as a litmus test. I thought my pastor and his wife wouldn't respect me or even think I was a Christian. I felt free to tell them that I had a hard time praying, even that I cheated on a chemistry exam! But I didn't feel free to discuss what was really going on with me sexually." A community working toward chastity is not captive to euphemism, dissembling, and pretense, but is a place where sin can be spoken of freely, with contrition, but without fear.

Another mark of a community working toward chastity and nurturing single people is good speech about singleness, for our assumptions about singleness are reflected even in the seemingly innocent language we use to discuss it. Judging by the vocabulary of many Christians, unmarried churchgoers are an afterthought: author and editor Debra Farrington has pointedly asked why we call twenties and thirties fellowship groups "pairs and spares." I have often wondered why we use "single" as a noun. Perhaps no marker of identity should be a noun other than Christian, since that is the most fundamental identity any of us claim. Everything else could be relegated to adjective: North Carolinian Christian, blonde Christian, fat Christian, Norwegian Christian, male Christian, married Christian, single Christian.

Then there's that mysterious term *call*. We've all heard (and many of us have asked) that dreaded question: "Lord, am I called to lifelong singleness?" This is usually followed by a protest. And it is sometimes followed by "How do I know?"

It's good language, the language of call, when linked to either marriage or singleness. It reminds us that our social, familial, emotional, and sexual arrangements are not simply about us—they are foremost about God, about the one doing the calling; and they are also about our community, the community that helps us discern and live out these callings. The language of call reminds us that the choice to marry, or to join a convent, or to stay single sans monastic vows, is about more than merely making a choice.

I once heard a pastor address the question, how do I know if I am called to lifelong singleness? His answer: if being single is not hard for you, if you are able to do it easily, then you might have a call to remain single forever. This is a reasonable word on discernment as far as it goes; we are generally called to the things God has gifted us in, and that gifting often translates into a certain ease and desire. Calls to professions or jobs offer a useful analogy: I am quite certain I am not called to be an architect, because spatial relations are impossible for me. If I were asked to read blueprints for a house, I would find no joy or ease. But many of us are called to things that we do not always find easy. I may be called to be a writer, at least right now, but

I often find writing to be the hardest thing in the world. And ask most married people whether they think "gifting" equals "ease"—they may feel they have been called to be married, but not too many married couples will tell you marriage is easy. I think these burdens are part of the fall.

Perhaps we ought not fixate on *the call to lifelong singleness.* Some people, of course, are called to lifelong singleness, but more of us are called to singleness for a spell, if even a very long spell. Often, our task is to discern a call to singleness for right now, and that's not so difficult. If you are single right now, you are called, right now, to be single—called to live single life as robustly, and gospel-conformingly, as you possibly can. The problem comes when the assumption that these are lifelong callings creeps in—panicked single folks think they must discern, at some given age on some given date, whether or not they are called to singleness forever. Again, consider professional callings. We are often called to certain vocational or professional paths for periods of time—one is called to be a doctor or a teacher or a waitress, but to discern a call to go to dental school at age twenty-four is not to assume that one will be called to work as a dentist forever. Perhaps at thirty-five, one will be called to stay home with small children. Perhaps at forty, one will be called to open a stationery store. Perhaps at sixty-three, one will be called to retire. Indeed, even calls to marriage are often not lifelong—not because of divorce, but because of death. Jane may be called to be married to Peter right now, but if Peter dies, she will find herself called, for a season, to singleness—to widowhood.

Orthodox theologian Paul Evdokimov has stressed that discernment is always mysterious, tricky, careful work; we always see through a glass darkly. We should think of vocation as "an invitation, a call from the Friend. I accept it today in the contours of my present situation until the moment when I will *perhaps* see more clearly." A single person contemplating his future, says Evdokimov, should accept the "open, though still undefined, horizons" that stretch out before him, and he should not let fear push him to "control the freedom of the spirit." (This is wise advice, but I find it very hard to follow. I am a terminal J on the Myers-Briggs, so I love closure and plans. The open horizons and the freedom of the spirit sometimes make me very, very nervous.) "For the time being," writes Evdokimov, the single person "accepts *this situation* cheerfully, with joy; he views it as a task limited to today, as the present and the full value of his life."

This wisdom, I think, teaches us something about vocation and discernment in general—not just how to think about a call to singleness or a call to marriage, but how to think about a call to teach, or preach, or parent, or befriend. "[O]ne's vocation is found exactly on the crest between necessity and creative freedom, along the line of faith, which reveals the direction as its free and strong confession grows," says Evdokimov. "One's entire vocation is an option, an answer to a call that has been heard. It can simply be the present condition. It is never a voice that clarifies everything. The dimness inherent in faith never leaves us. There is one thing we can be sure of, that every vocation is always accompanied by a renunciation. One who is married renounced monastic heroism; a monk, the married life. The rich young man of the Gospel is not invited either to marry or to enter a monastery. He had to renounce his wealth, his 'having,' his *preferences*, in order to follow the Lord. . . . However, in all cases of deprivation Scripture speaks of, grace offers a gift; out of a negative renunciation it creates a positive vocation."

Amen.

A Community Where People of Different Ages and Stations Come Together

A community that works toward chastity is also a community that understands, supports, and embraces the single life. There is a trend in churches today to segregate people into demographic groups. Single twenties and thirties in one Sunday-school class, families with small children in another, empty-nesters in a third, senior citizens down the hall, and so forth. Indeed, many churches have "dealt with singleness" by starting singles' groups or singles' Bible studies, and hiring associate ministers who are charged with the task of ministering to single Christians.

I see the appeal of such groups, but I am cautious about them. Perhaps the most robust expression of Christian community comes when we connect people of all demographics, people who might not meet each other if left to their own devices—toddlers and senior citizens and married couples and single professionals and empty nesters. This may cut against the grain of the organizational flowcharts that have become de rigueur in so many churches, separating parishioners into market groups (though the intentional fostering of relationships across demographic lines does not necessarily preclude a thriving Bible study for single parishioners, or a young mothers' prayer group). I have never joined a church with a singles' group, not because I think they are horrible or suffocating, but because church has always been one of the very few places where I can meet and know people who are not superficially like myself—it is only in church that I get to know kindergartners, and elderly people, and young families. (Not to mention that Griff and I met at a church committee meeting where we were the only people this side of fifty—so of course we began to chat! If we'd been at a big singles' mixer, we might never have noticed each other.)

One of the best ways Christian communities can support chastity is to ensure that married people and single folks are in relationship with one another. Fostering relationships between married and single means not assuming that "couple" is the basic unit of Christian identity. It means asking the single person not only *who are you dating?* but *how is God calling you to be faithful now as you are?* It means making sure you have an odd number of chairs at your dinner parties.

Fostering relationships between single and married Christians can help with the old accountability saw. A dating relationship is not private affair—when you are dating, your friends ask you questions, and they won't let you hide behind vagueness and innuendo. But relationships require more than having honest heart-to-hearts with one another. Relationships require that married people must invite single people into their lives, and vice versa. This means not just inviting your friends over for dinner; it means going grocery shopping together and taking vacations together. It might even mean—as it does for Christians who create "intentional communities" in houses or neighborhoods—married couples or families with kids living with unmarried folks.

In Romans 12:1, Paul instructs the church to "offer your bodies as a living sacrifice." The grammar of that command is odd—we are offering bodies, plural, as one living sacrifice, singular. But that seeming grammatical slip, I think, tells us a lot about community, chastity, and prayer. Those who are not married *and* those who are married offer our bodies as a single, communal sacrifice to God. It is something we do together—as one Body.

The Theological Witness of Singleness

It is good, of course, to be sensitive to single people's feelings. But the primary reason to embrace and sustain singleness is neither therapeutic nor sociological. The church should attend to singleness, not because more and more adults are unmarried, but because singleness occupies a distinct and crucial place in God's economy.

The model of singleness par excellence—the figure who is unmarried and best illustrates a life well lived—is Jesus. To remember that Jesus never married is not to make some cute quip. For Jesus's singleness is not simply a reminder that life can be lived well as an unmarried person; it is rather a way into Jesus's radical teachings about marriage and families. One of Jesus's most basic challenges to first-century Judaism was a challenge to the order of family. When, in Mark 3, his own family comes to see him, he flatly asserts that his followers, not his biological kin, are his real family; and in Luke 9, Jesus instructs a recently bereaved son to forgo the obligation of burying his father in order to "go and proclaim the kingdom of God." This is not the stuff of "family values."

Jesus is not the only New Testament figure to question family. Paul—not to mention Augustine and most of the early church fathers—seems to think the single life, lifelong celibacy, is preferable to marriage. To be sure, Paul's views on marriage were shaped in part by his expectation that the end of time was right around the corner, and much of the early and medieval church's high praise of celibacy was infused with disdain for sex, women, and bodies in general. But their preference for singleness cannot be dismissed merely as a product of misguided eschatology or antiquated misogyny.

To the contrary, the centuries of robust endorsement of chastity—and concomitant wariness about marriage—are good reminders that singleness and marriage are like the interleaved pages of one novel; both states teach us, the community of the church, some important truths about God's story.

What Marriage Teaches the Church: "God's Love Actualized among God's People"

If you'd known Yvonne and Jeremy Circleton when they were in their thirties, you would have said they were destined for divorce. Put plainly, they couldn't stand each other. It was widely known that Yvonne had cheated on Jeremy with at least two different men. And even if that was mere rumor, people whispered, it was clear the couple was mismatched. Jeremy was a corporate lawyer, he worked around the clock, and his great desire was for a second home in the south of France (though no one understood this, since he never took a vacation). Yvonne was a weaver. She was also a great cook. She loved film. She couldn't stand her husband. She used to say that her love for him had died on the vine.

No one but Yvonne and Jeremy know exactly what happened—and perhaps even they don't know. People were praying for them. Gradually things began to turn. They still get a little tetchy with one another, but now, in their midforties, they have an enviable, admirable marriage. (Still no house in the south of France, however.)

When I see them, I not only feel optimistic about the plausibility of staying married, I also feel optimistic about the plausibility of staying a faithful Christian, of not drifting from church when I grow bored or indifferent or angry. I remember that the Bible tells me over and over that marriage is like the relationship between God and His beloved. I am cheered.

The Circletons' marriage is doing exactly what it is supposed to do. In the Christian grammar, marriage is not only for the married couple. Insofar as marriage tells the Christian community a particular story, marriage is also for the community. Marriage presupposes fidelity, and married people are a sign to the church of God's own radical fidelity toward all of us. He loves us, and is faithful to us, when we cheat on Him. He loves us, and is faithful to us, when we insist that our love has died on the vine. Marriages are made in part to remind us of God's relentless fidelity.

And marriage tells the church about the communion and community that is possible between and among people who have been made new creatures in Christ. It hints at the eschatological union between Christ and the church. As ethicist Julie Hanlon Rubio has put it, "Marriage consists not simply or even primarily of a personal relationship. Rather, it crystallizes the love of the larger church community. The couple is not just two-in-one, but two together within the whole, with specific responsibility for the whole. . . . They must persevere in love, because the community needs to see God's love actualized among God's people."

The inflections of community are important because they get at the very meaning of marriage. Marriage is a gift God gives the church; He does not simply give it to the married people of the church, but to the whole church, as marriage is designed not only for the benefit of the married couple. It is also designed to tell a story to the entire church, a story about God's relationship with and saving work among us.

What Singleness Teaches the Church: "Vacancy for God"

Singleness instructs the church in other lessons just as vital. Singleness tells us, for starters, of a radical dependence on God. In marriage, it is tempting to look to one's spouse to meet all one's needs. But those who live alone, without the companionship and rigor of marriage and sex, are offered an opportunity to realize that it is God who sustains them. Catholic writer Henri Nouwen suggests that this dependence is the unmarried person's primary witness to the married. In singleness, says Nouwen, "God will be more readily recognized as the source for all human life and activity. . . . The celibate becomes a living sign of the limits of interpersonal relationships and of the centrality of the inner sanctum that no human being may violate." Unmarried people are asked to specialize in "creating and protecting emptiness for God," an emptiness that everyone, married or single, needs to maintain. This, perhaps, is why Aquinas spoke of celibacy as a "vacancy for God."

In singleness we see not only where our true dependence lies, but also who and what our real family is. Singleness reminds Christians that the church is our primary family. In an era in which the church is known for promoting "family values" but not social justice, in an era in which families are so exhausted from an endless round of after-school ballet lessons and late-night work-related e-mail sessions that they sleep through Sunday morning worship, in an era when middle-class Americans hurtle across exurban sprawl in our SUVs and then zip through our subdivisions and into our garages without ever speaking to our neighbors, this is a very important lesson indeed.

Marriage, and families, can be sources of grace, but they are not the primary source of grace. The primary source of grace is the church. Single people witness to the Christian hope that the kingdom of God unfolds not principally when we nurture our nuclear families, but, as theologian Stanley Hauerwas explains it, when we show "hospitality to the stranger. . . . As Christians we believe that every Christian in one generation might be called to singleness, yet God will create the church anew."

Perhaps most important, singleness teaches us something about eternity. One of the passages of scripture that happily married people like least is Matthew 22:23–30, in which a band of Sadducees comes to Jesus and asks him about a woman who had married, and survived, seven different men. At the resurrection, the Sadducees wanted to know, whose wife would she be? Would she have seven husbands in heaven? Jesus replies, "At the resurrection people will neither marry nor be given in marriage."

This rankles many husbands and wives not only because they adore their spouses, but also because we Christians believe that in heaven, in the Great Hereafter, we are resurrected and known as particular people; our resurrected selves are, in fact, our very truest, realest selves. If our particular loves and relationships are part of what makes us who we are as particular persons, what does it mean for us to be stripped of our most essential relationships, those of husband and wife, in heaven? Am I not, in my very essence, at the level of my very being, the wife or husband of the person to whom I am married?

It's a vexing teaching. It's a hard teaching. I often find myself with the first-century crowd who, Matthew tells us, heard Jesus's reply to the Sadducees and was "astonished at his teaching."

The teaching is astonishing, but it is clear. Jesus's reply to the Sadducees teaches us not only something about marriage but also something about the resurrection. And singleness hammers home Jesus's lesson. At the end of time, there is only marriage between Christ and the church. Jeremy Circleton won't be Yvonne's husband, and I won't be Griff's wife.

Single Christians remind the rest of us that our truest, realest, most lasting relationship is that of sibling: even husband and wife are first and foremost brother and sister. Baptismal vows are prior to wedding vows. (Inversely, insofar as marriage is essentially an opportunity to learn, in concentrated form with one other person, what being a sibling in Christ means, married people can instruct single people in some slices of the sibling relationship.)

Marriage and singleness remind us of and resonate with different moments in God's relationship to His people. As St. John

Chrysostom wrote, marriage "is the image of heaven," and celibacy is the image of the kingdom, "where there is no marriage." Married people—as the frequent scriptural analogies between marriage and Christ's relationship to His church make clear—mirror God's relationship with His people eschatologically. At the end of time, when the kingdom of God is consummated, when Christ returns, there will be a huge wedding feast between Christ and His people. Paul gets at this in Ephesians 5: "'For this reason a man will leave his father and mother and be united to his wife, and the two will become one flesh.' This is a profound mystery—but I am talking about Christ and the church. However, each one of you also must love his wife as he loves himself, and the wife must respect her husband." The church, as a collective people of God, become the Body of Christ. Marriage, in this way, instructs the church in what to look for when the kingdom comes—eternal, intimate union.

And singleness prepares us for the other piece of the end of time, the age when singleness trumps marriage. Singleness tutors us in our primary, heavenly relationship with one another: sibling in Christ.

9

RESPONDING
TO M.

The Practicalities of Repentance

The New Testament makes clear that God forgives us *before* we can show evidence of our change to the good, and claims that this gift of unconditional acceptance is what makes our transformation possible. Forgiveness is no empty decree, but the renewal of personal union with Christ. Out of this closeness, we look for the changes that Christ can bring about. In repentance, we are first and foremost exposing our lives to the action of grace, allowing Christ to enable us to do what our unaided moral efforts cannot hope to accomplish.

—Martin L. Smith

Recently a friend of mine—a 25-year-old single man whom I'll call M.—wrote me an e-mail about sex. M., a med student who became a Christian a few years ago, had met a woman at a coffee shop. They chatted, and then she scribbled her address on a napkin and said, "If you're not doing anything late-ish on Friday night, drop by." M. knew this was a proposition, no question about it. He e-mailed me to ask why he should pass up the opportunity:

> I know that as a Christian I'm not supposed to have sex before marriage, but you and I both know I've already *had* sex before marriage. Why shouldn't I have sex if I'm already "used goods"? Confessing that I didn't have my "quiet time" this morning is much easier than "Last night I had a few drinks and went home with this girl and we had that wild sex that was great. In addition, I really don't feel too bad about it and am kind of hoping I run into her again next Friday."
>
> Also, why should I wait if God forgives anyway? I mean I've already had sex with several women, so what's the difference? I've often heard that you should "save yourself" for your wife, that remaining a virgin will make you a better husband. I'm apparently already destined to be a lousy husband, so what does it matter if I have sex again a few more times?
>
> Let's face it, sex is so easy to get. At UNC alone, there are multiple opportunities for me to have sex. I'll quote a girl I met at a party the other night. Thursday morning I check my e-mail. She's e-mailed and basically said something like this: "Tonight I'm going out with some friends and going to have some drinks. Give a call tonight if you are free. Perhaps I'll let you come take advantage of me." Then there is this: "I find you intelligent and different from most other guys. You have a standing invitation to come sleep with me whenever you want." No questions, no commitment, no anything except a good night of sex. There are times when I hear a sermon that deals with the chaste ethic that we Christians are called to, and, as new creatures in Christ, capable of . . . and that same night hang out with a girl that heard the same sermon and we get sexual and sensual.
>
> I'm dealing with seventeen other things in my Christian walk. Shouldn't I just focus on learning to pray, and deal with the sex stuff later? I became a Christian as an adult—i.e., after I was already "sexually active"—and now have to deal with the fact that I already have a mark against me before I even got out of the starting gate.

Responding to M.

For some folks, maybe, practicing chastity isn't centrally about repenting for past willful sin. A widowed or divorced person may have a long road of adjusting to life without sex, but her task may not require repentance per se. For many of us, however, inhabiting our sexuality *as Christians* will require our acknowledging sin (even if that sin is "merely" lust) and beginning repentance.

Sin, as we discussed in chapter seven, is real and formative. Just look at the book of Proverbs. Its motivating tool is the destructiveness of sin. Proverbs does not lay out rules, but rather describes reality—the reality of sin—as it is: *If you go with this adulterous woman, you go to the grave.* It is this insight into sin that animates J. R. R. Tolkien's discussion of darkness in *The Lord of the Rings*: the trees, the water, the whole of civilization is threatened because of a dark power.

But to say that sin is formative is not to say that sin—sexual, or any other stripe—is unforgivable, nor that sin's consequences can't be undone or redeemed. Too often, the church seems to suggest that sexual sin cannot be forgiven: M. has every reason to wonder if he should bother with sexual discipline. We hear from the pulpit and read in the pages of magazines and books that "sexual experiences don't ever go away totally. They live on, like ghosts, in all future relationships, and can do real damage there." We learn that premarital sex "can scar a marriage for a lifetime." We read that if we have premarital sex, then, come our wedding day, the specters of the other men or women we slept with will hover around our betrothed.

This language of scars and ghosts suggests that sexual sin is wholly different from any other sort of sin. That its consequences last forever. That somehow, Jesus's saving work on the cross does not cover this.

All of those suggestions, of course, are patently false. "As far as the east is from the west, so far has he removed our transgressions from us." As the prophet Isaiah promises, though my sins are red as scarlet, I can be made white as new snow. And that applies to scarlet-red sexual sins, too. In *Mere Christianity*, after dwelling at length on sexual morality, C. S. Lewis chastises the Christian who would suggest that illicit sex is the singular unforgivable sin. "If anyone thinks that Christians regard unchastity as the supreme vice, he is quite wrong. The sins of the flesh are bad, but they are the least bad of all sins. All the worst pleasures are purely spiritual: the pleasure of putting other people in the wrong, of bossing and patronizing and spoiling sport, and back-biting; the pleasure of power, and hatred. . . . [Thus] a cold, self-righteous prig who goes regularly to church may be far nearer to hell than a prostitute."

There is, to be sure, a tension: sexual sin forms us. It teaches us false lessons about what sex is, lessons that are not easily unlearned. (I find that in my marriage, I still have to do battle with my expectation, formed through years of premarital sex, that sex is always supposed to be exciting.) But sexual sin is something we can repent of. It is something God forgives. It is something that can be washed away, bleached a startling white. Sexual sin teaches us lessons about sex, lessons that take time, community, prayer, and the Holy Spirit to unlearn. But repentance works here just as it works anywhere else. M.—should he repent, should he "turn and sin no more"—would not be damaged goods. He would, instead, be a Christian living faithfully.

Thinking about Our Vocabulary, Part One: Secondary Virginity

You might have noticed that thus far, I've not talked much about virginity. The emphasis that Christians sometimes place on virginity may be, to put it bluntly, destructive. In some Latino communities, men are so determined to marry virgins that Latina women are undergoing hymenoplasty, a surgical procedure that reconstructs the hymen, allowing women to "relive"—that's the verb choice of one woman who underwent the surgery—virgin sex. (A noteworthy example of the confusions of our culture: I first read about hymenoplasty in an issue of *Latina*; the same magazine cover that asked "Your Virginity: Would You Pay to Get it Back?" also screamed, in even larger letters, "Get Sexy: New Hair Looks and Daring Colors for Your Curves.") On the island of Crete, hymenoplastys are also popular—gynocologists there perform the surgery two to three times a week.

Many Southern belles have decided to reclaim their virginity, too, albeit without the aid of surgery. In recent years, engaged women who were happy to have sex while dating have insisted on periods of chastity before the wedding day. Lauren Ward, a bridesmaid whose betrothed friend gave up sex for a few months before her wedding, explained, "I've grown up thinking that you're not supposed to sleep together, but since everyone does, you stop when you get engaged for two or three months just before the wedding. I'll probably do it. Just for the tease." In other words, a period of enforced chastity can spice up a honeymoon that threatens to be ho-hum. (How exciting is your wedding night if you've already had sex 1,002 times?) "We decided it would be better to hold off till the wedding night so it would be new and exciting," said a groom in Birmingham, Alabama. "We originally planned for eight weeks and then decided it was too long, so we did it for four weeks. The wedding night and the honeymoon were definitely better." The men like the practice not just because it ensures fireworks on the honeymoon, but because, as one groom's sister put it, "It fulfills their fantasies of marrying a Southern belle." These self-rejuvenating virgins (to borrow the phrase one cynical commentator used) have not so much rededicated themselves to the holy discipline of chastity, but have rather contorted it to utilitarian ends. They aim to get something they want—Scarlett O'Hara, an unforgettable wedding night—rather than to become the way God wants them to be.

Some sociologists suggest that the rejuvenated virgin bride is a secular Southern imitation of the Christian "born-again virgin." These "born-again virgins," or "secondary virgins," are those unmarried Christians who've had sex, but who have rededicated themselves to chastity. The concept—turning from

sin, rededication to righteousness—is a good one, but the ter-
minology, which became popular about a decade ago, is silly. It
tells us less about the born-again virgin himself, and more about
the communities that emphasize a one-time state, virginity,
rather than an ongoing unfolding of discipleship, repentance,
and faithfulness.

To organize one's Christian sexual ethics around virginity
is to turn sexual purity and sexual sin into a light switch you
can flip—one day you're sexually righteous, and the next day,
after illicit loss of your virginity, you're a sinner.

This is not to say that there's not something special and
wonderful about being a virgin on your wedding night. Indeed,
one who, like me, had sex before marriage can rightly mourn
and grieve the loss of virginity. It is rather to say that the critical
question for Christians is *what are you doing now?* Not *have
you sinned in the past,* but *if you sinned in the past, how are
you dealing with it? How has Christ's blood redeemed you,
and how are you obeying now?*

Thinking about Vocabulary, Part Two: Purity

Here's a snapshot of a popular Christian abstinence program,
usually aimed at high-schoolers. The teens stand up in a line or
circle. A few of them are handed Cheetos or Doritos to munch,
and everyone is given a cup of water. Each teen takes a swig
of water, swishes it around her mouth, spits the dirty water
back into her cup, and then pours a bit from her cup into her
neighbor's cup. The defiled cups with their Cheetoish saliva
are meant to represent the body, contaminated by STDs and
generally defiled by premarital sex.

I thought of this abstinence program a few Sundays ago
when I was serving at my church as a chalice bearer, one of
the lay people who offers the cup to the body of believers during the service of Holy Communion. I have served as a chalice
bearer since the month after my baptism, and it has always
been my favorite, most treasured aspect of church service. On

the Sunday in question, though, I got grossed out. For the first time since I began serving communion, I noticed, as Mrs. J. handed the silver chalice back to me, that there was a giant rivulet of saliva running down into the cup. I did not have a holy, sanctified thought. Instead, I thought "Gross! I am going to have to drink that saliva," because—in order not to waste the consecrated wine, the blood of Christ—the chalice bearer always consumes any wine that might remain in the chalice once everyone else has been served.

Back at home, as I was still shivering at the thought of the saliva I'd swigged, I found myself juxtaposing the two cups—the teenagers' cups of spit, signifying the body defiled by misordered sex, and the silver chalice of spit-laced communion wine, signifying the Body of Christ.

It is easy to misread Paul's words to the Corinthians about joining your body with a prostitute. His point is not that Christians should not join their bodies to prostitutes—to the contrary, we are called to do that very thing. The point for the Paul is the manner of joining. *We are not to join our bodies to prostitutes through sex; we are, rather, to join our bodies with prostitutes—and with all other repentant sinners—in the Body of Christ, in the sometimes germy communion cup.*

And so we might probe the way the contemporary church throws around the word "purity." Purity is, of course, a biblical category, and biblical writers spend a lot of energy around purity. But in the New Testament, concerns about purity are reconfigured. This is why Jesus sees lust as such a problem. For Him, the problem is not, as in the Hebrew purity codes, that we become dirty by touching someone dirty, but rather that we become dirty by lusting after someone in our hearts. The fact of being connected to a prostitute per se is not the basis of the impurity; the impurity comes when I consume another person as merely a source of satisfaction. We can, in this sense, make anyone into a prostitute. C. S. Lewis's self-righteous prig may make a prostitute of his own life. By this standard—the standard of lust—not a one of us is sexually pure. We are all broken and fallen and in need of forgiveness and restoration. Of course, we need not banish the word *purity* from our lexicon. Purity is a good word, an old word. *Chaste* simply means *pure*. (We can talk about water as chaste—in fact, in the Canticle of the Sun, St. Francis of Assisi does just that.) The problem comes in trying to isolate purity in relation to sex, and in isolating sex itself as an index of what it means to be pure. In my church, Christ Episcopal Church, we regularly say a prayer called "the collect for purity":

> Almighty God, unto whom all hearts are open, all desires known, and from whom no secrets are hid: Cleanse the thoughts of our hearts by the inspiration of thy Holy Spirit, that we may perfectly love thee, and worthily magnify thy holy name; through Christ our Lord.

To practice sexual chastity is not to guarantee our own personal purity or righteousness. It is rather to strive to do sex, to have relationships with other people, and to comport our bodies and our desires in ways that perfectly love God and worthily magnify His name.

The Reconstruction of a Culture

We find one answer to M.'s questions in Paul's letter to the Colossians. "Since, then, you have been raised with Christ," writes Paul, "set your hearts on things above, where Christ is seated at the right hand of God. Set your minds on things above, not on earthly things. For you died, and your life is now hidden with Christ in God. When Christ, who is your life, appears, then you also will appear with him in glory." As many commentators have pointed out, these verses are a bridge in the middle of Paul's letter connecting the first chapters, which deal principally with belief, to the last chapters, which deal principally with ethics and behavior. In fact, these verses are both a bridge and a summary of the entire Christian message.

We Colossians, we Christians, have been cut off from God through sin. But, as Paul tells us earlier in the same epistle, "When you were dead in your sins and in the uncircumcision of your sinful nature, God made you alive with Christ." Our death has been undone by Jesus's death. "Since, then, you have been raised with Christ, set your hearts on things above, where Christ is seated at the right hand of God." Now we are alive in Christ; now we are "hidden with Christ in God"; now we can begin the work of living the Christian life. (Put grammatically, the imperative follows the indicative.) But this is no mere ethics. It is rather about eternity. For "when Christ, who is your life, appears, then you also will appear with him in glory."

The next verse in this passage of Colossians is one of the oft-quoted Pauline imperatives about avoiding sexual immorality: "Put to death, therefore, whatever belongs to your earthly nature: sexual immorality, impurity, lust, evil desires and greed, which is idolatry. Because of these, the wrath of God is coming. You used to walk in these ways, in the life you once lived. But now you must rid yourselves of all such things as these: anger, rage, malice, slander and filthy language from your lips. Do not lie to each other, since you have taken off your old self with its practices." We seek to do right because we fear the wrath of God, but more centrally because we have died to sin and have been given a new self. As the Reverend Mark Ashton has put it, "It's as though there were two volumes to my life as a Christian. The first volume of my life, in which I have been living, God has closed. And He's opened a second volume in which I am now living. And there are things which belong in Volume 1 which have no place at all in Volume 2. God shut that first volume. He closed it. He forgave those things and I am finished with them because I am now living in Volume 2. And I need to . . . leave them behind as no longer being a part of the life that I've entered into with Christ."

M. is only periodically convinced by the apologetics of chastity; sometimes he believes that God really cares whether or not he has sex, and sometimes he doesn't. When I got his e-mail, I suspected that another fifteen-minute lecture on Genesis and Paul wasn't going to be adequate to the task. So here is what I finally said to M.: "Do this as a favor to me. Don't go to that woman's apartment; just this Friday, pass it up—and know that Saturday morning I'm going to call and ask what you did last night." Of course, I could call and ask and M. could lie to me, but I don't think he will. Granted, asking M. to refrain from premarital sex as a favor to me is not endlessly sustainable. But it is the beginning of the church's being a community to him, a community whose members act on faith, in trust, even if we don't understand or believe or feel convinced right that minute.

M.'s e-mail is a reminder. Sometimes adopting chastity is as simple as reading a book like this one, or attending a lecture, and then making a change in your life. But for many of us, it is the relearning of a basic story. It requires prayer, teaching, work, reformation, even weeping. It requires that we tell each other the story of the gospel, and the narrative of chastity, over and over and over. To embrace chastity is to reconstruct a culture, and the reconstruction of a culture doesn't happen overnight.

What M. is struggling with is not so much sex as repentance. The Greek word for repentance is *metanoia*, and it means "to change one's mind," "to feel remorse" or "to rue," and ultimately "to convert" or "to experience a conversion of life." Under M.'s questions lurks the suspicion that sex doesn't really matter, that God doesn't really care what M. does with his body. And coupled with that suspicion is the destructive rhetoric of the church whenever it acts as if sexual sin is the worst sin there is. The truth is found in the middle ground: sexual sin is not unforgivable, but neither is bodily behavior unimportant.

In his e-mail, M. wondered how to balance giving up sex with the seventeen other things he's trying to do as a Christian—he's trying to learn to tithe, and to pray, and also to respect his mom. Why should he struggle to give up sex? It is a fair enough question, for sex is not the most important thing on the planet. But to think of spiritual formation as seventeen discrete things is already to sidestep the point. The gospel, after all, is not a compartmentalized approach to God, but rather an engagement in love. The questions Christians ask are not "Do I have the energy to deal with sex/prayer/gossip this week?" but "What is the whole duty of man? What does it mean to be wholly converted?" To be sure, we don't attain perfection overnight, but repentance begins a process that reaches into every part of our lives. The image of Christ in us is holistic, and what we do with one hand (pray, love our mom, give away money), we can undo with another. And of all seemingly isolated activities, surely sex is the least separate: it is communal, and intimate, and embodied, and social, and its consequences are communal, intimate, embodied, and social, too.

The process of *metanoia* is not merely a process of growing into a list of dos and don'ts, but rather an increasing recognition that you have earned nothing that you have—not your life or your body, not grace, not salvation. It is a process of learning to live thankfully (or, if you will, eucharistically, the word *eucharist* deriving from the Greek for *thanksgiving*).

Christian lives are ordered around a response to God of gratitude for the life He sustains and redeems in us, and that response of gratitude affects all the different parts of our lives. Who am I in relation to this God whom I now acknowledge as my creator, redeemer, and sanctifier? It is not what I do so much as what God has done and how I am responding to it.

There is a reason, I think, that my own dawning awareness of sexual sin began with the rite of reconciliation. To confess my sin to a brother or sister—whether or not that confession happens in formal sacramental space with a member of the clergy—is to unfold my sin in the hearing of a godly person who can meet me on my level, talk to me about it, and assure me of God's forgiveness. Most of us live, after all, in relative ignorance—we speak in ignorance, pray in ignorance, and have sex in ignorance, because we are not awake; because our moral lives are not well enough formed to know whether the shape they are taking is right or wrong, gray or black or white. Confession puts us in the company of people who can speak truth in love to us, about our sin, about the need for amendment of life.

Amendment of life is the essence of the thing. My priest will not speak the words of absolution to me if he does not believe that I intend to change. When we confess our sin, we see that the question is not what we've done and who we've been, but how we are dealing now with what we've done and who we've been. The desire to amend our lives is inseparable from conversion. Conversion and a sense of *metanoia* are required for us even to begin to talk about matters as weighty and entangled as sexual sin and forgiveness. But Christians are a people of *metanoia*, and *metanoia* people are concerned with something more than the immediate value of a thing; we are concerned with more than fulfillment for its own sake. We want fulfillment as a way of celebrating and giving thanks to God for the gift of life and for the natural things that draw persons together. We want to be like the One who made us.

This doesn't mean we won't fall short—we all fall short. But we can place ourselves in a posture of awareness. We can confess sin, individually and corporately. We can receive counsel and assurance from fellow Christians, who can speak God's absolution to us. We can send away our sins.

Sending away our sins is important because the sins are destroying us.

And sending away our sins is important because a sin that is forgiven is forgiven. It is gone. We may not unlearn overnight the lessons that sinning taught over years, but we no longer have to *do* the sins. We can abandon sinning. We can set it aside. The power of Jesus's forgiving the adulterous woman is that when he says *Go and sin no more*, His forgiveness makes it possible for her to do just that.

Picture forgiveness by remembering the way our parents taught us to swim or walk. They didn't get behind us and shove us forward into the world. Rather they stood in front of us and beckoned us toward them. Our Lord does the same. He stands in front of us and says "Come to me." He beckons us, and we can reach for Him.

NOTES

Chapter 1: Unchaste Confessions: Or, Why We Need Another Book
about Sex

9   *Confession . . . sin is still possible.* Stacey D'Erasmo, "Northern Expo-
    sures" (review of *The Haunting of L*), *New York Times Book Review*,
    April 21, 2002.

10–11   *"Since we've never . . . they've shaken hands."* Jan Karon, *A Light in the
        Window* (New York: Viking, 1996), 144.

16   *About 65 percent . . . finish high school.* http://marriage.rutgers.edu/Pub-
     lications/SourcesThings4Teens.htm

16   *websites like hotornot.com . . . casual sexual escapades.* Benoit Denizet-
     Lewis, "Friends, Friends With Benefits and the Benefits of the Local Mall,"
     New York Times Magazine, May 30, 2004.

16   *A 2002 Study . . . cohabited with a man.* Centers for Disease Control
     and Prevention. "Cohabitation, Marriage, Divorce, and Remarriage in
     the United States." Vital Health and Statistics Series 23, Number 22,
     Department of Health and Human Services, 2002.

16   *Fifty-two percent . . . 75 percent have sex before they get married.* "Women
     by the Numbers," *Esquire* (April 2002): 82.

16   *According to a 2002 study . . . part of a "casual relationship."* April Witt,
     "Blog Interrupted," *Washington Post Magazine* (August 15, 2004): 12–17,
     25–30.

16   *Three surveys of single . . . two-thirds were not.* Julia Duin, "No One
     Wants to Talk About It," Breakpoint Online, October 7, 2002.

16–17   *Recently professors at . . . ninth for men.* Judith Newman, "Proud to be
        a Virgin," *New York Times*, June 19, 1994.

   17   *True Love Waits, a popular . . . non-pledging peers to use birth control.*
        Diana Jean Schemo, "Virginity Pledges by Teenagers Can Be Highly Ef-
        fective, Federal Study Finds," *New York Times* (January 4, 2001). Susan
        Dominus, "The Way We Live Now: 1-21-01; Abstinence Minded," *New
        York Times* (January 21, 2001). Diana Jean Schemo, "Saving Themselves;
        What Teenagers Talk about When They Talk about Chastity," *New York
        Times* (January 28, 2001).

17–18   *In 2003, researchers at . . . to be sex.* "Teens break no-sex vows, study
        suggests; some say oral sex not sex," *Christian Century* (December 27,
        2003): 14. See also a telling letter to Christian advice columnist Tim Staf-
        ford. The teenaged writer notes that "Many of my friends have decided
        it's okay to have oral sex with whomever they're dating." Tim Stafford,
        "Love, Sex and Real Life," *Campus Life* (January/February 2003): 60.

   18   *Luke Witte, an evangelical . . . before the couple ties the knot.* Quoted in
        Elizabeth Hayt, "It's Never Too Late to Be a Virgin," *New York Times*
        (August 4, 2002).

   18   *The woman who writes . . . study the Bible.* Amy Elhoff, "The 'Porn
        Myth' Construct," *Vanderbilt Hustler*, November 4, 2003.

   18   *In 1992, flagship . . . 75 percent were Christians at the time of the affair.*
        Haddon Robinson, "Sex, Remarriage, and Divorce," *Christianity Today*
        (December 14, 1992).

18–19   *A recent study of teenage . . . dropping the ball.* Ethicist Amy Laura
        Hall generously shared this datum with me. She originally found it at
        www.dadsanddaughters.org

   20   *A careful reading of . . . address this problem directly."* Richard Hays, *The
        Moral Vision of the New Testament* (San Francisco: Harper San Francisco,
        1996), 372.

   21   *Lewis Smede's* Sex for Christians *. . . no memory of chastity.* Lewis B.
        Smedes, *Sex for Christians* (Grand Rapids: Eerdmans, rev. ed. 1994), 108.
        The 1994 edition includes a new epilogue, but the main text is true to the
        1976 edition.

Chapter 2: Real Sex: Creation, Scripture, and the Case for Sex in Marriage

   29   *Good sermons . . . doctrines of scripture.* Jeremy Taylor, *The Rules and
        Exercises of Holy Living*, excerpted in Thomas K. Carroll, ed., *Jeremy
        Taylor: Selected Works* (New York: Paulist Press, 1990), 456.

30–31   *We must do more . . . but as good news.* Thomas E. Breidenthal, "Sanctify-
        ing Nearness," in Charles Hefling, ed., *Our Selves, Our Souls & Bodies:
        Sexuality and the Household of God* (Cambridge: Cowley, 1996), 45.

   34   *I fashioned their members . . . strength of my thoughts.* Quoted in Susan
        A. Harvey, "Embodiment in Time and Eternity: A Syriac Perspective," in
        Eugene F. Rogers Jr., ed., *Theology and Sexuality: Classic and Contem-
        porary Readings* (London: Blackwell, 2002), 6–7.

34 *"the body and its . . . life must take place."* Wayne Meeks, *The Origins of Christian Morality: The First Two Centuries* (New Haven: Yale University Press, 1995), 16.

35 *Ambrose, bishop of Milan . . . from the beasts."* Ambrose of Milan quoted in Karen Lee-Thorp and Cynthia Hicks, *Why Beauty Matters* (Colorado Springs: NavPress, 1997), 200.

35 *As early as the first . . . sleep or food.* Meeks, 130.

36 *"The concept of the body . . . image of the body.* John A. T. Robinson, *The Body: A Study in Pauline Theology* (London: SCM, 1955), 9. Though I cannot enthusiastically endorse Robinson's later *oeuvre*, I heartily commend *The Body*, which is a clear, concise, and nuanced treatment of the use of the term *soma* in the Pauline epistles. Robinson is especially helpful in trying to understand why Paul is often thought of as someone who hates the body. Where does that bad rap come from? Robinson explains that "body" and "flesh," though seemingly synonymous, are not identical for Paul. When Paul contrasts flesh with "spirit," he is not simply reiterating the old Greek distinction between matter (evil) and spirit (good). Rather, for Paul "flesh" is something of a metaphor that suggests reliance upon the law, human knowledge, and so forth. See also Peter Brown, *The Body and Society: Men, Women, and Sexual Renunciation in Early Christianity* (New York: Columbia University Press, 1988).

36–37 *Meeks has captured . . . but of sin."* Meeks, 133.

37 *"where God has . . . find us in our fallenness."* Harvey, 9.

37 *Bodies are central . . . abiding with Him.* Harvey, 3–4.

37–38 *In a graphic speech . . . stops and the other's starts.* See Philip Turner, "Limited Engagements," in Philip Turner, ed., *Men and Women: Sexual Ethics in Turbulent Times* (Cambridge: Cowley, 1989), 56.

39 *You are stately . . . vines have budded.* Song of Songs 7:7–8, 12 (NRSV). The Song of Songs, of course, can be read on many different levels. The church has historically read the Song as not only a picture of human love but also as a picture of the relationship between Christ and the church. For an excellent discussion of the many layers of the Song, see Ellen F. Davis, *Proverbs, Ecclesiastes, and the Song of Songs* (Philadelphia: Westminster John Knox, 2000), 231–302.

39 *This term crops up . . . implication of prostitution."* Mark D. Jordan, *The Ethics of Sex* (London: Blackwell, 2001), 25.

40 *"If unmarried sexual intercourse . . . unmarried people is sin."* Smedes, 108.

Chapter 3: Communal Sex: Or Why Your Neighbor Has Any Business Asking You What You Did Last Night

43 *Salvation in Christ . . . member of God's people.* William Willimon and Stanley Hauerwas, *Lord, Teach Us: The Lord's Prayer and the Christian Life* (Nashville: Abingdon Press, 1996), 87.

44–46 *"a long garment of dark . . . was (or wasn't) Fabian's mistress.* Barbara Pym, *Jane and Prudence* (New York: Harper and Row, 1981), 121–124.

48   *"Bob's words had been . . . none of their business."* Danielle Crittenden,
      Amanda Bright @ Home (New York: Warner Books, 2003), 191.

48–49 *For most of human history . . . practice of sex.* Philip Turner, *Sex, Money,
      and Power* (Cambridge, MA: Cowley Publications, 1985), 30–31.

49   *"Sex, like any other necessary . . . is everybody's business."* Wendell Berry,
      Sex, Economy, Community, and Freedom (New York: Pantheon, 1992),
      119.

51   *"Brothers, if someone . . . the law of Christ."* Galatians 6:1–2.

52   *Character—the making . . . shared story, is impossible."* James Davison
      Hunter, *The Death of Character: Moral Education in an Age without
      Good or Evil* (New York: Perseus, 2002), 227.

55–56 *an idea called the household . . . it was a place of genuine mutuality.* On
      households, see McCarthy, *Sex and Love in the Home: A Theology of
      the Household* (London: SCM, 2001), especially pages 85–108. See also
      David Matzko McCarthy, *The Good Life: Genuine Christianity for the
      Middle Class* (Grand Rapids, Brazos, 2004), 72–76.

57   *Berry wants us . . . couples dance alone."* See Berry, *Sex, Economy, Com-
      munity, and Freedom,* 120, and Wendell Berry, *The Unsettling of Amer-
      ica: Culture and Agriculture* (San Francisco: Sierra Club Books, 1986),
      117–118.

59   *It is to ask the church . . . we do what we do.* See Catherine M. Wallace,
      For Fidelity: How Intimacy and Commitment Enrich Our Lives (New
      York: Knopf, 1998), 142.

Chapter 4: Straight Talk I: Lies Our Culture Tells about Sex

61   *Sexual delight, sexual drive . . . just about endlessly.* Wallace, *For Fidelity,*
      25.

61–63 *In May 2004, Jessica Cutler . . . I'd talk about it in graphic detail with
      my friends."* April Witt, "Blog Interrupted," *Washington Post Magazine*
      (August 15, 2004): 12–17, 25–30.

63   *over 14,000 . . . in his or her lifetime.* Sari Locker, *The Complete Idiot's
      Guide to Amazing Sex* (New York: Alpha Books, 2002), 9.

64   *"as effective as the Pill . . . It's that simple."* *Vogue* (December 2003):
      96–97.

64   *Only recently have . . . endorsement of birth control.* Two useful resources
      on Protestants and birth control are Jenell Williams Paris, *Birth Control
      for Christians: Making Wise Choices* (Grand Rapids: Baker, 2003), and
      Bethany and Sam Torode, *Open Embrace: A Protestant Couple Rethink-
      ing Contraception* (Grand Rapids: Eerdmans, 2002). Thanks, as ever, to
      Amy Laura Hall for helping me think about the place of contraception
      and procreation in a gracious Christian sexuality.

65–67 *Christian tradition has historically articulated . . . every sex act need not
      be.* I am still in the early stages of rethinking Protestantism's twentieth-
      century embrace of birth control. I intuitively believe we Protestants
      have some rethinking to do, but where we land after all that rethinking
      is not yet clear to me. It seems that we need not end up at either of the

extremes of the *Vogue* ad or the *Humanae Vitae*. (I applaud the Orthodox Jewish model of managing contraception. Orthodox Jews are allowed to use birth control, but they are not allowed to make decisions about contraception individually. Instead, a married couple meets annually with their rabbi, and the three decide together whether the couple ought to use contraception for the next six to twelve months. This model is not only judicious, it is also communal. It implies a recognition that even intimate decisions about sex and family are not, finally, "private" decisions, but decisions in which the community has authority.) For good Protestant defenses of birth control that hinge on the idea that over the course of a marriage, sex needs to be open to procreative and unitive functions, but that not every sexual act need be open to procreation, see James Nuechterlein, "Catholics, Protestants, and Contraception," *First Things* 92 (April 1999): 10–11. Indeed, the Catholic insistence that each and every sex act be open to procreation may ironically be connected to the broader culture's idea that each and every sex act is supposed to be mind-blowingly orgasmic and feel emotionally transformative. In each stance, we see a narrow scrutiny of each single sex act, as though each sex act can be isolated from the household, from the domestic warp and woof in which it plays out. Neither view seems able to understand married sex not as a series of discrete incidents but rather a years-long unfolding.

68–69   *A columnist in the* Washington Post *. . . argue with such motivation."* Philip D. Harvey, "Adulthood without Sex," *Washington Post*, May 12, 2002.

69   *We want to make sure . . . replicate their parents' mistake.* http://abcnews .go.com/sections/wnt/WorldNewsTonight/wnt010629_marriedlater_fea- ture.html. See also Frederica Mathewes-Green, *Gender: Men, Women, Sex, Feminism* (Ben Lomond, CA: Conciliar Press, 2002), 99–106.

74   *"Menswear is moving much faster . . . more comfortable with it."* Tom Ford, quoted in Shaun Cole, "Ford, Tom," http://www.glbtq.com/arts/ ford_t.html.

75–76   *A Sears, Roebuck . . . judge me on what I wear."* Leslie Kaufman and Cathy Horyn, "More of Less: Scantier Clothing Catches On," *New York Times*, June 27, 2000.

77   *Hard work . . . all by itself."* Pepper Schwartz, *Everything You Know About Love and Sex Is Wrong: Twenty-Five Relationship Myths Redefined to Achieve Happiness and Fulfillment in Your Intimate Life* (New York: Perigee Books, 2001), 110.

77–78   *"They do not have . . . more than bordello."* Sue Monk Kidd, *The Secret Life of Bees* (New York: Penguin, 2002), 115.

78   *At the same time . . . just a game.* For a discussion of popular culture's insistence that "Sex is easy; sex is free; and sex can be engaged in with any willing partner," see Jenell Williams Paris, "The Truth about Sex," *Christianity Today*, November 2001.

78–79   *For amid the contradictory messages . . . head to a B & B.* David Matzko McCarthy, *Sex and Love in the Home: A Theology of the Household* (London: SCM, 2001), especially 1–64, 213–217.

79 *Or they could, as one bride's guide . . . spice things up.* Marge Stark, *What No One Tells the Bride* (New York: Hyperion, 1998), 178–202. See also Lauren F. Winner, "In Search of the Good Marriage," *Books & Culture,* September/October 2004.

79–82 *This notion of sex . . . middle of things."* McCarthy, *Sex and Love in the Home,* especially 1–64, 213–217.

81 *Human intimacy is hammered out . . . struggles of love in the home."* McCarthy, *Sex and Love in the Home,* 43.

Chapter 5: Straight Talk II: Lies the Church Tells about Sex

85 *Christians should . . . that is, more theologically.* Mark D. Jordan, *The Ethics of Sex* (London: Blackwell, 2001), 2.

86 *"Because I felt so safe . . . tender entwinement of love."* All from Karen Bouris, *The First Time: Women Speak Out about 'Losing Their Virginity'* (Emeryville, CA: Conari Press, 1993).

86–87 *"Both my parents . . . think anything of it."* In a 1992 study, 40 percent of sexually active Canadian teens said they had experienced no guilt about having sex. C. Hobart. (1992). "Young Canadians, sex, and AIDS," *Youth and Society* 23, no. 4: 411.

87 *To understand that sex . . . people are about it."* See also Dallas Willard, *The Spirit of the Disciplines: Understanding How God Changes Lives* (San Francisco: Harper San Francisco, 1999), especially 158–159.

90–91 *One Christian marriage guide . . . it's difficult to define."* Bill and Anabel Gillham, *He Said, She Said: Building the Bridges of Communication in Marriage* (Eugene, OR: Harvest House, 1995), 145–148.

91 *"What Girls Need to Know . . . boy's lies or lines."* Tim LaHaye, *Raising Sexually Pure Kids: How to Prepare your Children for the Act of Marriage* (Sisters, OR: Multnomah, 1998), 161–170.

91–92 *For much of Western history . . . they didn't crave sex.* Nancy F. Cott, "Passionless: An Interpretation of Victorian Sexual Ideology, 1790-1850," *Signs: Journal of Women in Culture and Society* 4, no. 2 (1978): 219–236.

92 *Judith Wallerstein . . . evenly matched in desire."* Judith S. Wallerstein and Sandra Blakeslee, *The Good Marriage: How and Why Love Lasts* (New York: Warner Books, 1995), 190. See also Michelle Weiner Davis, *The Sex-Starved Marriage: Boosting Your Marriage Libido, a Couple's Guide* (New York: Simon & Schuster, 2003), especially 4, 60–62.

92 *Over 57 percent . . . as we want."* Laurie Sandell, "5 Truths about Sex Now—Exposed," *Glamour* (March 2004): 126.

92 *"Teenage girls today . . . deeply aggressive creatures."* Sharon Lamb, *The Secret Lives of Girls: What Good Girls Really Do—Sex Play, Aggression, and their Guilt* (New York: Free Press, 2001), 7–9.

92 *It is worth noting . . . circumstance and life stage.* Wallerstein and Blakeslee, 190.

94 *You were bought . . . glorify God in your body."* 1 Corinthians 6:20 (NRSV).

96 *"You have so carefully . . . repulsive at first."* Douglas E. Rosenau, *A Celebration of Sex for Newlyweds* (Nashville: Thomas Nelson, 2002), 123.

96 *"Some women bring . . . Yes!' after marriage.* Lisa Graham McMinn, *Growing Strong Daughters* (Grand Rapids: Baker, 2000), 167. Doug Serven, a campus minister at the University of Oklahoma, put the matter more colorfully to me in an e-mail: "Some of my students take Pharisaical pride in their virginity. . . . They pledged their virginity to Josh McDowell and will present that to their husbands on their wedding days. And, about a year later they hate sex and are dying."

97–98 *Books like* Intimate Issues *. . . gourmet sex a month.* Linda Dillow and Lorraine Pintus, *Intimate Issues: 21 Questions Christian Women Ask about Sex* (Colorado Springs: Waterbrook, 1999); and Douglas E. Rosenau, *A Celebration of Sex: A Guide to Enjoying God's Gift of Sexual Intimacy* (Nashville: Thomas Nelson, 2002).

98 *A 1994 study . . . religious affiliation at 22 percent.* Mark Oppenheimer, "In the Biblical Sense," slate.msn.com/id/56724/.

99 *Twenty percent . . . once a month.* Davis, *Sex-Starved Marriage,* 4.

99 *The problem is also . . . plunged into routine.* See McCarthy, *Sex and Love in the Home,* 34.

99–100 *Either we live as angels . . . satisfaction of the organism."* Walker Percy, *Lost in the Cosmos* (New York: Noonday Press, 1992), 192.

Chapter 6: On the Steps of the Rotunda: Line-Drawing and Formation

103 *Legalism fails . . . encourage obedience.* Philip Yancey, *What's So Amazing About Grace?* quoted in Jeramy Clark, *I Gave Dating a Chance* (Colorado Springs: Waterbrook, 2000), 26.

104 *Theologian . . . or is it not?"* Christopher West, "Introduction," *Pope John Paul II, Body and Gift: Reflections on Creation* (adapted by Sam Torode) (South Wayne, WI: Philokalia Books, 2003), x.

106 *They've grown up on television . . . parsing and spin.* "Teens break no-sex vows, study suggests; some say oral sex not sex," *Christian Century* (December 27, 2003): 14.

109 *"a purposeless virtue . . . have practical justification."* Berry, *The Unsettling of America,* 121.

111 *one survey suggests . . . regularly use Internet porn.* "Caught in the Porn Trap," http://www.oneby1.org/resources/porn_trap.html

111 *another study, conducted in 2000 . . . at least once.* Dirk Johnson and Hilary Shenfeld, "Preachers and Porn," *Newsweek,* April 12, 2004.

111 *One pastor's wife . . . pulpit Sunday morning.* Lauren Winner, "The Next Big Challenge for Clergy," http://www.beliefnet.com/story/61/story_6116_3.html

112 *This is well illustrated . . . telling what in his mind,"* Clyde Edgerton, *Raney* (New York: Ballantine Books, 1997), 211–213.

112–113   *In a* New York *magazine . . . act like porn stars.'"* David Amsden, "Not Tonight, Honey, I'm Logging On," *New York Magazine*, October 20, 2003.

113   *Feminist critic Naomi Wolf . . . just bad porn."* Naomi Wolf, "The Porn Myth," *New York Magazine*, October 20, 2003.

115   *"Masturbation is difficult . . . the world from God's perspective."* Tim Stafford, "Love, Sex and Real Life," *Campus Life* (June/July 2003): 58.

116–117   *"[O]ne of the things . . . experience you'd like."* Doug Roberts, "What Sex Feels Like for a Man . . . When He's Home Alone," *Glamour*, February 2003.

117   *in the same* New York *. . . "substitute for reality."* David Amsden, "Not Tonight, Honey, I'm Logging On," *New York Magazine*, October 20, 2003.

117   *"sex," unadorned . . . sex before marriage.* See McCarthy, *Sex and Love in the Home*, 44–45.

118–119   *The main story our society tells . . . allows sex to be what it is.* McCarthy, *Sex and Love in the Home*, expecially 1–64, 213–217.

119–120   *("I'm 33 . . . making a home movie.")* Vanessa Grigoriadis, "The New Position on Casual Sex," *New York Magazine*, January 13, 2003.

120   *Magazines are full of advice . . . rhythms of marriage.* McCarthy, *Sex and Love in the Home*, especially 1–64, 213–217.

120–121   *"And now it was . . . but very satisfying.* Alexandra Marshall, *The Court of Common Pleas* (Boston: Mariner Books, 2001), 87.

Chapter 7: Chastity as Spiritual Discipline: Conforming Your Body to the Arc of the Gospel

123   *Chastity . . . familiar with God.* John Climacus, *The Ladder of Divine Ascent*, Colm Luibheid and Norman Russell, trans. (New York: Paulist Press, 1982), 176.

125   *As Willard explains . . . also to those gifts."* Dallas Willard, *The Spirit of the Disciplines: Understanding How God Changes Lives* (San Francisco: Harper San Francisco, 1999), 92, 156. Italics deleted.

125   *But as I began to doze . . . stay awake one hour?"* See also the description of the vigil in Kristin Ohlson's excellent memoir, *Stalking the Divine: Contemplating Faith with the Poor Clares* (New York: Hyperion, 2003), 181–182.

128   *A woman of the early . . . temptations from us."* Benedicta Ward, ed., *The Desert Fathers: Sayings of the Early Christian Monks* (New York: Penguin, 2003), 27.

128   *Of course, the desire . . . refraining from something normal.* Dallas Willard, *The Spirit of the Disciplines*, 158–159, and passim.

129   *Dressing modestly . . . modesty protects and inspires."* Wendy Shalit, *A Return to Modesty: Discovery of the Lost Virtue* (New York: Free Press, 2000), 172–173.

130   *Working with the premise . . . both body and soul."* St. John Chrysostom, *On Marriage and Family Life* (Crestwood, NY: St. Vladimir's Seminary

Press, 1997), 105. Thanks to Molly Bosscher Davis for directing my attention to Chrysostom's wise book on marriage.

130   virginity "of the flesh . . . concern of all." Augustine, quoted in Paul Evdokimov, *The Sacrament of Love* (Crestwood, NY: St. Vladimir's Seminary Press, 1997), 170.

Chapter 8: Communities of Chastity: What Singleness Teaches the Church

133   *I have community . . . vital between us.* Dietrich Bonhoeffer, *Life Together,* John W. Doberstein, trans. (San Francisco: HarperCollins, 1954), 25–26.

134   *In the words . . . called to live chastely."* http://www.maristseminary.org.nz

135–136   *The most recent census . . . burgeoning unmarried population.* Michelle Conlin, "Unmarried America," *Business Week* (October 20, 2003): 106–116. "Marital Status of the Population 15 Years Old and Over, by Sex and Race: 1950 to Present," U.S. Census Bureau, 2001.

136   *Lana Trent . . . and alienate singles."* See Lauren Winner, "Solitary Refinement," *Christianity Today,* June 2001.

136–137   *"In my church," . . . its valued daughters."* Camerin Courtney, *Table for One: The Savvy Girl's Guide to Singleness* (Grand Rapids: Revell, 2002), 37–39.

138   *author and editor . . . "pairs and spares."* See Winner, "Solitary Refinement."

139–140   *Orthodox theologian . . . a positive vocation."* Paul Evdokimov, *The Sacrament of Love,* 96–99.

142–143   *One of Jesus's . . . proclaim the kingdom of God."* A both-and to the created order. Jesus's life is eschatological and opens up a radical dependence on God and a human community without marriage. On the family in the New Testament, see Julie Hanlon Rubio, *A Christian Theology of Marriage and Family* (New York: Paulist Press, 2003), 46–64.

143   *Paul—not to mention . . . bodies in general.* New Testament scholar Richard Hays suggests that Paul's eschatological framework "enables us to look to the future in trust and hope, knowing that our salvation depends not on our success in restructuring the world but on the vast mercy and justice of God," and that we can find our identity in Christ, not in a social category. Richard Hays, *First Corinthians* (Louisville: Westminster John Knox Press, 1997), 133. On the patristics and medievals, see, *inter alia,* Jordan, passim, and Lisa Sowle Cahill, *Sex, Gender, and Christian Ethics* (New York: Cambridge University Press, 1996), 121–216, and Cahill, *Between the Sexes: Foundations for a Christian Ethic of Sexuality* (Philadelphia: Augsburg Fortress, 1985), 105–138.

144   *"Marriage consists . . . actualized among God's people."* Rubio, 38. See also David Matzko McCarthy, "Becoming One Flesh: Marriage, Remarriage, and Sex," in Stanley Hauerwas and Samuel Wells, eds., *The Blackwell Companion to Christian Ethics* (London: Blackwell, 2004), 276–288.

145 *Catholic writer Henri Nouwen . . . "vacancy for God."* Henri Nouwen, *Clowning in Rome: Reflections on Solitude, Celibacy, Prayer, and Contemplation* (New York: Doubleday, 2000), 43–47. Aquinas quoted in Nouwen, 43.

145 *In an era . . . speaking to our neighbors.* See McCarthy, *The Good Life,* 72–76.

145 *Single people witness . . . create the church anew."* Stanley Hauerwas, *After Christendom?* (Nashville: Abingdon Press, 1991), 128. See also Hauerwas, *A Community of Character: Toward a Constructive Christian Social Ethic* (Notre Dame, IN: University of Notre Dame Press, 1981), 189–191.

146–147 *As St. John Chrysostom . . . is no marriage."* St. John Chrysostom, quoted in Paul Evdokimov, *The Sacrament of Love,* 101–2.

147 *"'For this reason . . . must respect her husband."* Ephesians 5:32–33.

Chapter 9: Responding to M.: The Practicalities of Repentance

149 *The New Testament . . . cannot hope to accomplish.* Martin L. Smith, *Reconciliation: Preparing for Confession in the Episcopal Church* (Cambridge: Cowley, 1985), 51–52.

151 *"sexual experiences . . . do real damage there."* Tim Stafford, "Love, Sex, and Real Life," *Campus Life,* January/February 2002.

151 *"can scar . . . marriage for a lifetime."* Brian and Heather Jamison, "Haunted by Premarital Sex," *Marriage Partnership,* Spring 2001.

151 *"As far as the east . . . our transgressions from us."* Psalm 103:12.

151 *As the prophet Isaish . . . white as new snow.* Isaiah 1:18.

152 *"If anyone thinks . . . than a prostitute."* C. S. Lewis, *Mere Christianity* (New York: Macmillan, 1960), 84–95.

152–153 *In some Latino communities . . . Colors for your Curves."* Mireya Navaro, "The Immaculate Deception," *Latina* (March 2004): 102–103, and cover.

153 *On the island of Crete . . . three times a week.* Dana Hudepohl, "Orgasm Secrets from Around the World," *Marie Claire* (December 2004): 126.

153 *Many Southern belles . . . self-rejuvenating virgins.* Elizabeth Hayt, "It's Never Too Late to Be a Virgin," *New York Times,* August 4, 2002.

154 *Here's a snapshot . . . defiled by premarital sex.* Judie Kinonen, "Teens get clear call for chastity from churches, new programs," *Christian Chronicle* 57, no. 11, November 2000. Diana Jean Schemo, "Sex Education With Just One Lesson: No Sex," *New York Times,* December 28, 2000.

155 *I got grossed out . . . germy communion cup.* Thanks to Amy Laura Hall for helping me articulate this point.

156–157 *"Since, then, you have been raised . . . with its practices."* Colossians 3:1–4.

157 *"It's as though there were . . . entered into with Christ."* This reading of Colossians leans heavily on a sermon preached by the Rev. Mark Ashton, The Round Church at St Andrew the Great, Cambridge, England, November 9, 2003.

ACKNOWLEDGMENTS

Many, many friends and colleagues read drafts of this book, and each improved it immeasurably. Thanks to Linda Beail, Mary Bosscher, Jerusha Clark, Camerin Courtney, Molly Bosscher Davis, Amy Laura Hall, Kelly Jennings, Sarah Johnson, Kathy Keller, Jill Lamar, Chuck Mathewes, Ken Myers, Enuma Okoro, Jennifer Conrad Seidel, Doug Serven, and Charles Smith. Conversations with Nathan Jennings, a scholar of asceticism, were crucial for chapter six, and conversations with the Reverend Brian Vander Wel and the Reverend Greg Thompson were crucial for the whole book (and, indeed, crucial for the whole living of my spiritual life). Conversations with Julia Duin, Derek Kruger, and Gene Rogers were also invaluable.

For research help and general wisdom, thanks to John Bailey, Cindy Crosby, Jonathon Kahn, Charles Smith, Beth Vander Wel, and David Vaughan. Matt Mutter helped me understand the brilliant Walker Percy.

Carol Mann proved her mettle, yet again, as agent and confidant. LaVonne Neff, who copyedited this manuscript, remains the sharpest and most elegant person in publishing. The good folks at Brazos and Baker Publishing Group were somehow simultaneously indulgent, stern, and generous, and I am very, very grateful; special thanks to Dwight Baker, Rebecca Cooper, B. J. Heyboer, and visionary editor Rodney Clapp.

You might have noticed that writers and scholars always single out their spouses in book acknowledgments, saying that without husbands and wives who converse and read and distract and prod and are willing to cook dinner every night for weeks, books would never get written. Now I understand what these acknowledgers are getting at. (I never did before. I thought it was just this expected thing you had to write in your acknowledgments.) So final thanks to Griff Gatewood, who had the foolhardy temerity to go on a date with, and then marry, a woman who was writing a book about chastity.

AUTHOR'S NOTE

When I write autobiographically, I strive for two things that are sometimes in tension: scrupulous factual precision and scrupulous respect for other people's privacy. Here, if I've erred, it is on the side of privacy. Many of the people who appear in this book (most obviously, but not exclusively, those with letters for names) are literary approximations of real people. I've at times created composites; and throughout, I've changed not only names, but also identifying details, all in the interest of sharing true stories without trespassing on anyone else's wish not to have his or her story known.